CONFESSIONS OF A HOLLYWOOD UBER DRIVER

BY
DAVID ASHLEY

PUBLISHED BY
TWIN ROAD

Table of Contents

PROLOGUE

The morning after a one night stand, on their way to an audition they probably won't get, somebody's late for work, on their way to take the L-SAT, first day at a job, the biggest interview of their life, leaving a failed gameshow attempt, on their way to a first date, first time in the city, first time back since moving, leaving a funeral, a celebrity that doesn't want to be noticed, an influencer who acts like she doesn't want to be noticed, girlfriends on their way back from brunch, awkward comment to their sibling mid ride, the mid-trip realization that the relationship is over, the realization that they've put in the wrong address, the timid husband trying not to gloat after a victory, the terrified wife scared of correcting her husband, the obtuse racist, the sex worker put in the car by her "manager", the quiet parent who knows that they can't control their child, the overwhelmed parent just seconds from a breakdown, silence after there's almost an accident, or when Spiderman and dirty Superman are fighting on Hollywood blvd, or when the driverless car is waiting for the delivery robot to cross the street before it can make the right turn, when you've found the courage to say "good morning", after a tense start to the ride and at least for a moment the energy has shifted. 30,000 trips and 30,000 stories.

Everybody has had their share of creepy, reckless, mean Uber drivers, but the interest passengers would show from hearing things from my perspective, it made me think that other people would like to hear these stories as well. Thank you for being here. You could be anywhere in the world but you're here with me and I appreciate that.

1

The Stats

At the time of this writing, I have 30,025 trips as an Uber driver. In those 30k plus rides, 70% were single person rides, another 20% were double occupancy or Uber-pool, another 8% were at least three people and the other 2% were four people.

When you break that down, I've had approximately 44 to 46,000 passengers I've driven around. That's 46,000 hellos, goodbyes, and too many miles, stoplights or turns to count. That's 44-46 thousand attitudes, lives, stories, personalities, troubles, heartbreaks, etc.

How many broken hearts have I helped or hurt? How many people who had just gotten the worst news of their lives, did I prejudge based on their mood? How many failed tests, confused students or abused spouses have I driven around?

How many people have I driven around who have just been assaulted, who have committed crimes, murders, have almost been murdered, have since been murdered or who had thoughts about harming me? It's bone-chilling. I count myself fortunate to have touched so many lives. I feel regret for those people who I didn't give grace to in the moment. I'm also grateful for the grace permitted me. Each chapter consists of a main story and an observation. You're about to go on a ride. Let's get it!

Chapter 1:
"I'm Gonna Ask You One More Time"

One day in LA I was driving on Sunset Blvd toward UCLA campus when I get a trip that took me to the Trader Joe's in Westwood. I arrived and a Middle Eastern man, between 25 and 30, carrying a paper bag from Trader Joe's and wearing what seemed to be a satchel or some sort of bag across his body, before they were trendy. I also noticed that he looked exhausted, but it mattered none because as soon as he got in the car, we started chatting it up quickly. We talked about family, traveling and Dubai, where he had family, and it was truly amazing just how quickly we started laughing about whatever.

Back then I was sort of new...so new that I was still playing the directions out loud over the speakers just so there would be no discrepancies or confusion about the route I was taking. The GPS took us down Hilgard, a street that outlines the eastern edge of the huge UCLA campus. Now we're at a light at Hilgard and Sunset, and once we cross Sunset, we are immediately in Bel Air, an even more lavish part of Beverly Hills. The moment we crossed over into Bel Air, the man who had been slouched as if tucked away in a Lazy Boy, sits up straight and yells, "WHERE ARE YOU TAKING ME!?". Confused, I slowed down the car. See, that entrance to Bel Air splits the street, and I turned left but maybe I made a mistake. I proceeded to make a three-point turn but before I could: "WHERE ARE YOU TAKING ME!?", he yelled again. I'm baffled and a bit flustered because on top of this being completely out of the blue, it's also loud and unhinged. It seemed othered-worldly, like something had taken over this person I was just laughing with. "I'm sorry, are you saying this because the route doesn't look familiar", I said.

"NO", he answered. "Do you know how to get there, I can take your directions", I said. "NO", he said, again. "Well, I'm sorry man, I don't know how to help you", I said. He yelled out again, "WHERE ARE YOU TAKING ME!?". I said, "My man, the directions are playing over the speaker, you're a grown man, where could I possibly be taking you?"

By this time, I've turned around and I'm going down the right side of the split street, and I've slowed the car down just in case I need to jump out. Then he reached down into his satchel and said, "I'M GOING TO ASK YOU ONE MORE TIME, WHERE ARE YOU TAKING ME?".

How are we here? We were just talking about how his sister accidentally took his passport and wallet on a flight with her, leaving him with no money or way to get home. How did It turn into such a frightening ordeal? If he was sitting next to me then we could get into some close quarters, bathroom stall, Jackie Chan movie fight scene type of action, not that I know any martial arts but that's just how it would look. But no, he's sitting in the back passenger side, and I've never seen anybody successfully punch backwards. It's not a real thing.

"MY MAN", I exclaimed, "Tell me where you want to go and I'll go there!", I said. "STOP THE CAR! STOP THE F*****G TRIP. THIS ISN'T COOL. IT'S NOT FAIR!", he said as I immediately obliged. With his right hand still in the bag holding God knows what, as if he has just robbed a bank and needs to keep a close eye on the patrons, he reaches across his body with his left hand and opens the door, grabs his Trader Joe's bag, kicks the door open and ducks out of the car - all with his hand still in the bag.

He takes a couple steps back from the car, then he turns around and walks off. I take off immediately to get some distance and once I feel safe, I take a deep breath. I'm done for the day.

4

I'm going home to watch an #11 seed beat a #6. (LOL) I'm not sure what makes someone switch that fast. I've asked so many people what it could have been, and I've gotten every answer from drugs to bipolar, most people settling on the latter. Whatever it was, it was severe and sudden. There could've been anything in that bag.

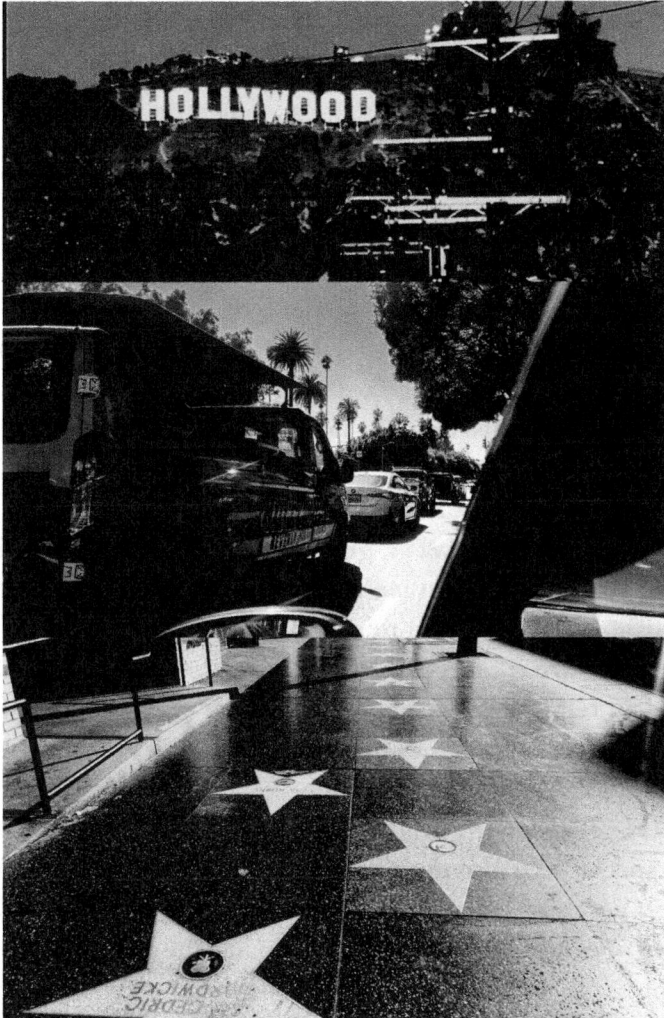

Why an Uber driver?

The short answer is that I'm an actor and a flexible work schedule is paramount for me. I worked at a start-up for five years, I had a great relationship with the owners, and they allowed me to audition. But when I was let go, the odds of me finding another job with owners who would let me audition, were slim to none... so, I bought a Prius, and I started driving Uber.

In hindsight I've found several things that I could've spent that 401k and severance money on, other than a car, that could've saved me from still being in that car a whole ten years later. At the time I was so blinded by the idea of being my own boss, that I wasn't paying attention to what I was actually craving, which was financial freedom.

How many vending, ATM machines or billboards could I have had by now, had I just taken a few more weeks to examine all my options? Truth is that I was in a new relationship, and this was uncharted territory for me, and I got tunnel vision.

I applied to Lyft first and on October 31st , 2014, I gave my first ride. My first fare was a guy going to CSUN (California State, Northridge). He wasn't driving because he had just recently gotten a DUI, had to pay $10,000 and had his license stripped. I drove with Lyft until I happened to give a Lyft ride to an Uber recruiter who then helped to onboard me because Uber was notoriously slow and impossible to work with back then.

Once I got to Uber I pretty much stayed there unless there was a special Lyft promotion that would give out a specific amount of money for a specific, not too hard to attain number of rides. See, Uber had most of the market share, probably still does. They came out immediately with the hard-core logo and were no nonsense.

6

We'll take you there and drop you off, whereas Lyft cars had these huge pink mustaches on them that made you question if you wanted to ride with them. I truly believe that's why Uber jumped out to such a lead, and I'm pretty sure that those things affected both the drivers they hired, as well as the clientele. At the beginning it was euphoric. I'm making my own money in my own time, and I can stop and start whenever I want?

This is amazing! Then there comes the realization that you must be a mean boss. After too many days off with no money coming in, the fun sleep-in days are over.

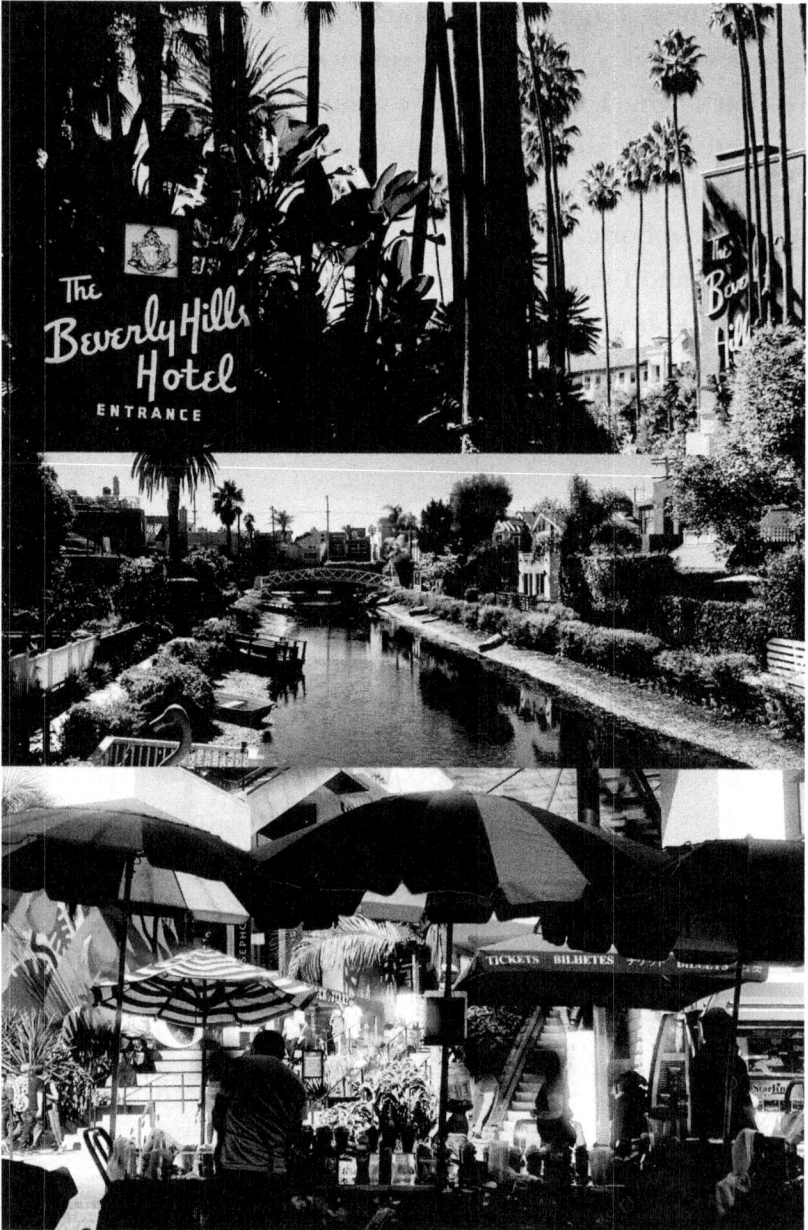

Chapter 2:
She Just Won't Wake Up

One night in downtown LA, I came across two women outside of a warehouse party. One of them could barely walk, the other was walking fine. I have a rule that unless you're a woman by yourself, if you can't walk to my car then I'm not giving you a ride. I've had too many regurgitations in my car. As I decided to leave, the street I turned onto made a short, weird U-turn and it ran me directly back into the women and it was too late to turn away. The sober(ish) woman carefully placed her very drunk "friend" into the car and closed the door. I assumed that she was going to get in on the other side but instead she tossed the girl's phone into the window, closed the door and said, "thank you", then she scurried back toward the warehouse party.

As the door closes, the drunk friend starts to hiccup. Lord. In between those hiccups she drunk-yells, "Where is my friend coming with us?". At this point I am 168% certain that she's going to throw up whatever liquor that fueled this behavior, all over my back seat. On our way she hiccups less and less and after about 10 minutes we're at her apartment, which was on the extended campus of USC where there is a mix of student and non-student housing.

When we pull up, I look at the back seat, and she's asleep. "Hey there, we're here", I said and nothing. I said it again, just a little louder this time and still, nothing. I honk my horn a couple of times; I step on the gas then the brake, to try and shake the car and nothing. I honk my horn a couple of times; I step on the gas then the brake, to try and shake the car and nothing. I try the combo of turning up the radio while semi-yelling, "hey HEY, we're HERE!", because maybe the change in volume will work – nothing.

I call her phone while calling her name, I call her name while smashing the brakes at the same time and still, nothing. She's scantily clad with a tiny dress and tube top so there is nowhere I can use to shake her with my hand and get her attention; besides, I tried this before on another trip and her eyes opened mid-reach, "WHAT ARE YOU DOING!?", she yelled. "I've been trying to wake you up ma'am, we're here", I said. "Oh, okay. THANKYOUBYE!", she said cheerfully. That was terrifying. No more touching.

Back to the present and this woman will not wake up. I got out of the car, and I opened her door and just stood there, hoping it would look like something other than a heavily bearded black man with an unconscious white girl in his back seat at 1:30 a.m.

I'm not scared but I am thinking of all the ways this can go wrong. She could wake up and scream bloody murder, she could technically still throw up, and I'd be at the mercy of whatever happens. It's just an unfortunate position to be in. It's uncomfortable and like a 12-year-old stuck at church, I just want to go home. We're so close because she's actually at her apartment, but so far because she is in a deep, drunken stupor.

Finally, I see a white van with USC written on its side. There's a young white man driving (think Napoleon Dynamite), and like a matador I dash in front of the van, risking my weighty midsection in an attempt to slow this van to a halt. He stops, looks at the car and the girl inside and nods his head. He understood. I urged him to call the campus police, and he did. I guess I could've called the police myself, but I just felt better about having someone else there as a witness.

The police arrived and they tried for five or ten minutes to wake her up to no avail. The cops then called the paramedics who arrived with two huge Optimus Prime looking ambulances. EMTs hop out and they try to wake her up for another five or ten minutes, also to no avail. "Welp", one of them exclaimed, "we're gonna have to pull her out". One pushed and the other pulled from the other side, until she was out. And she did throw up, but it was after they pulled her out of the car. She then stood up and started swinging at everybody before they subdued her and put her on a gurney.

"Everybody back inside", the officer said as he tried to leave me without proof that he was there. I said, "my man, I need something from you", He said, "It's okay, she's safe, you're good", interrupting my plea. "No, I need a card or an incident number, or something to help me", I said. He was almost disgusted that I insisted. "Please, as a favor to me", I said. Reluctantly he goes back to his car, writes something down and gives me the card. I was finally on my way home.

I got home and I laid down for about five minutes thinking about the night. Something just didn't feel right so I got up, and I emailed Lyft exactly what happened, cop card and information included. I went to sleep only to wake up the next morning to a call from Lyft explaining that the girl's boyfriend said that the girl said that she only had one drink and that she didn't know what happened and until they could "figure out what happened", that they'd have to suspend my account and investigate me...Dang, is right.

Two hours later they called me back frantically explaining that they had just read my email, that everything had been checked out and that I was reinstated.

They apologized to me, but I wonder what happens if I don't convince the officer to give me the card or if I don't send the email to Lyft. I'd be cooked, and who puts their very drunk friend in an Uber with a complete stranger at 1:30am?

THINGS I'VE SEEN/HEARD

One time in Inglewood I accompanied a woman who I was certain was a sex worker, and who was walked out to my car very closely by an overbearing "Supervisor". After about five minutes in the car, she picked up at least two phone calls from someone tracking her whereabouts and was trying to make sure she didn't make a run for it. It was eerie. I asked her, "are you okay?", and she answered with zero emotion, "yes". I said, "you sure?", and she answered with the same tone. I said, "you know if I end the trip then he can't see where we are anymore", to this she didn't even respond. I left it alone because what was I, captain save-em, going to do but get her in trouble? He called her three more times during our 10-minute drive.

Another time in Hollywood, I witnessed a man having either a psychiatric or a drug-induced episode. He was naked with socks on and there was a woman smiling, laughing, and filming him. Perhaps she was from out of town and hadn't seen this before. Then something in her clicked and she slowly put the phone down, took off her jacket, walked over to him and gave him her jacket to cover up. It was a gesture even the naked man wasn't quite ready for. It was beautiful in its sadness.

One day I heard a gay man on the phone say, "I'm not going to be your peace. If you want peace, then go be with your wife. This is adultery, da fuq?!". My flabbers were gasted, as they say.

I've witnessed a man have a woman dead to rights in an argument and twenty minutes later by the end of the ride, that same man was in the doghouse. She turned it around and the man who was up by 4 with 2.3 seconds left, somehow lost by 10 in overtime. It was masterful.

13

I witnessed a father dressed in USC everything from head to toe, grimace as I dropped off the family on the campus of UCLA. His daughter chose the enemy, and this was move-in day. He was disgusted that he had to tour enemy territory for hours with his daughter who was now a proud Bruin.

I've driven around two separate people who thought it was cool to do a bump of cocaine from a key, in the front seat of my car.

One day I picked up three white people at SONY studios... there were two men and a woman. I'm clearly an engager but I wasn't getting a talky vibe from them, so I said hello, and I thought I'd just listen to the radio for the rest of the ride. We sat in total silence for about 20 minutes before the woman broke the silence with, "Damn, Gary. Did you even study?", and the car erupted with laughter. I had no clue what she was talking about, and I still laughed. It turns out that Gary had just been a contestant on Jeopardy and had a terrible showing; he left with no money. This opened a flood of conversation and fortunately Gary was feeling a little better, at least for the moment.

Chapter 3:
Who Is Radiance Obama?

One day in LA I got a fare but when I arrived at the place, there were two buildings, so I parked in the middle. Sometimes the pin is different than where they intended to order from, and I don't want them to have to walk too far, just in case it's an older or disabled person. Plus, I like to get some kind of heads-up/view of where someone is coming from.

After two or three minutes a woman appeared; she was walking from behind me, on the passenger's side. I did a double take because she looked familiar. I looked at my phone to check the name, but it didn't match so I didn't think any more of it.

She was on the phone when she got into the car. Never breaking stride from the very engaged conversation, she whispered, "hi, yes", to me. Once I verified the name, I gave the thumbs up, and we were off. The conversation was rather spirited, and I always had a podcast going in my left ear bud, and since I never wear both, I took the left one out and put the right one in, just so I can hear better and block out their conversation.

We're about three or four minutes in when I hear her say, "I didn't want it to be all official, but they met my dad first". That could mean anything, but clearly it heightened my Spidey senses because I remembered it. A couple of minutes later she says, "no, Sasha will meet them before I do", and now I'm trying hard just to mind my business and focus on whatever podcast I'm listening to. I tried, I swear I tried, until a couple of minutes later she said, "Oh, no. You don't have to make a big deal out of it, like you don't have to say you're Malia's friend, or anything like that." Father God...

The eagle has landed!!! Radiance (Not you cuz. Hope all is well with you, though lol), but Radiance is in the Prius. I repeat, RADIANCE IS IN THE PRIUS!!! This ain't a drill and I do not know what to do! I have Barry and Chelle's first child in my care. And this sounds jokey, but my first thought was, "Black America won't be blaming me for fumbling this one". My hands are 10 & 2, everything by the book. I'm even thinking about talking into my wrist or collar just so people can know I'm not playing around, but I didn't want to freak her out.

My second thought was, "so this means that Secret Service has already looked me up and they know everything". Are they following me? Do they know where my Mama live, my cousins? Is there protocol? I work for the former President and First Lady now, I'm not even regular anymore, at least until I drop her off! The third thing I'm thinking is, "Do not look your goofy eyeballs into this rear-view mirror". It was so hard not to - LOL

I'm pulling out all the stops. I'm stopping short and pulling past cars next to me so that she doesn't have to look directly at anybody, I'm just making up stuff to make sure I'm doing right by The Obama's, and I'm positive that three secret service drones/suburbans are following me – not really, but why wouldn't there be? About 15-20 minutes later I got her to the destination, she hopped out of the car then opened the door back to apologize for talking on the phone, which people often do, but I wanted to tell her "I had health care because of your pops. You ain't got to apologize for nothing", but instead, I chilled. I just nodded and said goodbye. I had to log off for a few minutes after that one. I had to see if them boys were still watching. I guess I did okay but sheesh, the pressure! I got you, Barry and Chelle!

PASSENGER PET PEEVES

Sometimes the passengers and the drivers are on completely different wavelengths, so I just want to clear up some things, set some boundaries for your next ride with one of us.

Please don't vape in my car without asking. Matter of fact just don't vape in my car. If you're by yourself, don't get into my car and sit directly behind me, it's creepy. Also, if you're by yourself, don't get in the front seat. Ngl (I just used young letter slang), when I first started, having someone sit in the front made me feel less like a chauffeur, but now, especially since Covid, get thineself in the back seat! If somehow you think that your GPS is superior or you just don't trust the route that I'm taking, don't be so bold as to play your GPS out loud. I will stop the car if you don't mute it, I promise.

I understand that everyone isn't an engager like me. Not everybody wants to have a conversation, but unless you're deaf, don't speak English or have another issue that won't allow you to talk, you must speak to me in my own car. Again, we don't have to go past "hello", or, "morning", but I can't speak and not hear anything back from you.

Sometimes people want to be one step ahead and prove that they can follow the map, and they cross the street to try to meet me so that I don't have to make a U-turn. That's an amazing gesture but make sure you tell me if you're planning to do it, because now I must make yet another U-turn to now get to you on the other side.

This next one is near and dear to my heart. A big peeve for me is when a passenger gets in and asks; "oh, they're taking you THIS way?". MY GOD - I hate it so much. My answer is always, "is there a particular way that you want to go?", and most times they say, "oh, no. I was just wondering".

And I say, "I can go whichever route you want me to take", and most times they just fall back. Occasionally they chime in again after a few more turns with, "why are they taking you this way?", at which time I turn off the GPS, and I have them direct me for the rest of the trip. Truth is, only a very small number of people know an LA neighborhood well enough to truly give you an effective short cut.

First off, cover your mouth when you sneeze/cough. It's staggering the number of people who don't practice that as a rule. Unfortunately, the sneeziest and coughiest people always want the window rolled up. No. I won't be trapped with the fast and furious, 60mph germ particles whizzing through the closed window after you've snoze. (And yes, it is a word). I've had Covid twice and lord willin' I won't catch it ever again. I'll roll the window up a little bit, but not the whole bit. Nope.

Don't ask me, "Could you hurry, that'll help me a lot. I'm running late". No, that is the answer. "Is there another way that we can go?", during rush hour in the second largest city in America. No. We can't hurry and there isn't a short cut. Also, you know that text you send when you know it's taking you too long to get out to the car, it doesn't matter. You've got a timer that starts when I get there and at the end of those five minutes, that text matters none. Now, me, myself, personally, I call before I leave but please don't have us out there waiting for 6.7 or 8 minutes.

And lastly, please don't get in the car and play your super loud audio out of your phone. People play their loud phone noises, and it'll drown out the car radio and they're none the wiser. I just don't understand it. Folks' lack of spatial and situational awareness is either at an all-time high, or I'm just now noticing it. Okay. Rant over, thanks for listening.

Chapter 4:
"Sometimes I Get An Escort"

I get a fare in Beverly Hills. I pull up and it's an Asian man. Younger, around 27-28 years old. He's sort of arrogant but not rude. He had been in the car for about five minutes when I started hearing what sounded like whimpering. He kept doing it almost as if he wanted me to ask about it, "aaaawww, s**t man", so I asked. "You okay, man?", I said. "Man, I messed up, man", he whimpered. "Do you need me to take you back, did you forget something?", I said. He was silent, almost like he was suddenly occupied. Now I'm in, "do I need to get this dude out of my car", mode. "My man, are you okay?" I asked again. After about 10 seconds he says, "Sometimes I get an escort, okay?", as if I was Bill Duke in a smokey interrogation room.

What had been a confident, slightly cocky business owner had, in a flash, turned into a seventeen-year-old who had just crashed his dad's vintage Chevy. The turn was fascinating. "Okay", I said. "Nothing wrong with that", I reassured. "No, but I was going to have you drop me off at a bar in West Hollywood so that I could hang out with the guys and get more contacts, so I blew her off", he said, almost crying. "But now she's all mad and this is what she just texted me",

"I was really counting on that money. You're a grade-A a**hole, but it's ok, I know who would appreciate hearing this information", then he sent him a screenshot of his wife's name and cellphone number. "Wow, I see", I said. "Awww man, we just had a baby, and my wife is going to take everything!", he sobbed. Just then he got another text. "So, I'll expect to see you, that $700 plus a little tip downtown at the Standard in an hour, okay?".

19

He asked, "bro, can we change the destination?". I agreed and I changed the destination to the Standard, DTLA, which makes the trip 30-40 minutes longer, but I need to see how this plays out. Any minute now I'm expecting a film crew to pop out and tell me this is a new prank show.

Damn, how great of a google searcher do you have to be to pull that off? I've never gone to an escort but after this I'm never blowing off an escort (pause). I'll be there and I'll be on time, if ever the occasion comes. What would I do, how would I handle this threat? The things that must've been going through this guy's brain. Here he was, distraught in my back seat, seeing all he's worked for about to crash to nothing.

"What do you think I should do?", he asked. "You should pay her", I said, matter of factly. "But it's supposed to be discreet, she can't do that to me", he pouted. I said "bro, we're past that. You need to take her that money". "You're right", he said, "so you're taking me to the Standard, right?", he said. "Sure", I affirmed. "Wait, let me ask her what she has on, because I don't know what I'm walking into. Her pimp could be in there waiting to kick my a**", he said. "What should I say? Maybe I'll ask her what she has on, that way I can see her before she sees me", he said. He sends the text, and she texts back, "I'll be wearing black pants", "aww man, that could be anybody" he said. LOL It's not funny, but looking back, it's funny.

"No, you know what, this thing is supposed to be discreet. She can't do that to me, I know somebody who can do something to her", he said. "Dude! You're putting a problem on to another problem. Do you have the money?", I asked. "Yeah, I'm not broke", he said, "then pay her the money and get this problem out of your life". This calmed him down, realizing that this was the only way to go.

For the next twenty or so minutes he vacillated between being tough and how the exchange was going to go down, then he came up with an idea just minutes away from The Standard. "What if, because money isn't an issue, I could just, like just tell me what you want. I could, like, pay you to drop it off for me, if that's something you'd be cool with. I could pay you", and as the great actor Isaih Whitlock once said as the character Senator Clay Davis on the greatest show of all time "SHHEEEEEEEIIIIIIIID". I shot that idea out of the sky like a clay target. You want me to get swept up in the middle of their prostitution sting whilst you're outside in my running Prius? Nah, broski.

We pulled up to the Standard. It's a one-way street and as he was going to hop out on the back driver's side and into the doors of the Standard, he said, "I'll be right back out". I said, "oh, you want me to stay here?", "yeah, just in case I need to run back out", he said innocently. HA! Bro, although my Toyota Prius has a little turbo button, it is still a Prius and is not the car to be trying to escape in. The same way he didn't know what's going on in there, I don't know what's going on in there. I hope everything worked out for the young man, cuz I skirted off as fast as my turbo button would allow me to. The moral of the story is, well firstly, don't cheat on your wife, but secondly, pay that worker for their time.

WHAT WAS/IS UBER POOL?

To help prepare for the next story, I'll explain Uber Pool for you, just in case you aren't familiar. Uber pool (Lyft Line) was something they put together to pay us less under the guise of efficiency. The mission was to pick up one person and then pick up another person on the way to where you're already going and drop that person off. To explain I'll use the entire country as a scale. If I pick up James from Washington DC and he's going to California, but four minutes into the trip, Amy who's in Florida... she opens the app and she wants a ride to Texas. I would take a detour from trip to California, and I would go pick up Amy, then I'd drop Amy off along the way to Texas, then I'd finish driving James to California, and all of this for a lower price for the customers and less money for the drivers.

At first it worked. You still got paid less for double the work but at least they really did stick to the, "along the same route", theme, but after a while they did away with all geographical decorum, and they just started doing the most with the directions and those became worse and worse trips to take for the money. Double the work for the price of one ride. They were the worst. The first time I tried it was in Sherman Oaks, and I picked up two women who were pretty lively and had been drinking, not so much that there was a throw up threat, but they were giggly.

One sat in front, and one sat in back, which was already weird. The one who sat in front got flirty. I'm flattered. I got another fare, and the man was around the same age as the women. He had also been drinking. It was make-out at first sight for him and the young lady already in the back seat because, before you knew it, they were kissing, deeply.

23

The girl up front was blushing and laughing, partially embarrassed because we could hear the smooches. I hate to be a hater but after a while, (I'm probably a hater) I stopped the smooch fest. I couldn't see it, and I wasn't going to be smelling sex in my back seat. I just wasn't. Here is where I would place the shrug emoji if I didn't hate it with my entire heart.

Or there was the time where I picked up two Asian women who didn't speak English and as we arrived at the second location, two young white girls were walking out to the car and were wondering why there were already passengers in the car. Her mom had ordered the Uber for them and she picked the first, cheapest option on the app. Meanwhile the two Asian women were in the US for the first time and didn't even know what Uber Pool was. We finished the trip without an explanation because I'm only one-lingual. Till this day they probably still think I picked up extra people on their ride.

There were a lot of people who tried to cheat the system by picking the cheapest price then claiming they didn't know, but still trying to get dropped off first.

This one time, still at the beginning of the Uber Pool Era, I was in south LA and I picked up a Hispanic woman in her mid-50's. We were riding and I got another fare. One telltale sign that someone is concerned about their whereabouts is when they start turning their heads looking out of both sides of the car. Most people don't want to say anything and instead this is their survival response to what they're going through internally.

This was no different. As we are moving toward the second location, her head is on swivel and suddenly I can hear "NO, NO, NO" and then a BUNCH of aggressive, concerned Spanish words flying rapidly out of her mouth.

My "ma'am, ma'am, this is Uber Pool", meant absolutely nothing to her because everything I said was rebutted with, "NOOOOOOOOO, NO, NO, NO", and TADA, she doesn't speak English! I'm driving for blocks with her scolding me in Spanish and me not knowing how to comfort her. I'm wondering what if she thinks I'm kidnapping her. What if she makes a call to someone alerting them that she's being taken. I do NOT need a call from Jesus Neeson! I can't drive too fast because I'm in a neighborhood, but I can't drive fast enough to this location just so someone else can be a witness to what is going on. I really need to quit driving.

Luckily the second passenger, a young Mexican man, got into the car and was bilingual and the regular Jesus, heard my cry and against the backdrop of her screaming, "NOOOOO, NO, NO, NO", I asked the young man to please explain Ube Pool to her. He did, she calmed down to an embarrassed chuckle, "oh, oh, ho-ho-ho, ci, ci". And we continued the trip. Cristo!

26

Chapter 5:
"Don't Make Us Come Looking For You"

This one was harrowing. I was in east LA, and I picked up a couple of painfully innocent teenage kids who got in the back seat, then I stopped and picked up an older Hispanic man who had clearly been drinking... he sat up front. His nephew stuck his head in the car and said, "he's been drinking a lil bit so take care of my Tio". Tio means uncle in Spanish.

Shortly after I take enough turns to not remember how to get back where I came from, the phone freezes and it won't even restart. So not only do I not know who's getting dropped off first, but I also don't even know where I'm going.

I decided to ask the teens, "Do you know where you're going?", and with a shy shrug they both say a variation of "I don't know". "Can you just direct me to which way you think it is?", I ask, desperately. "Okay", one of them says with complete uncertainty. I set out toward the direction that the innocent teens pointed me in, and it led me to a highway.

"Do you know the exit?", I asked and here they go again, "I don't know". Keep in mind that I'm still trying to restart a phone to no avail. At this point the old man starts to hiccup and that familiar stench of post-drunk, pre-vomit beer breath is creeping through the air. Hey, God. Do you love me, at all? Because right now would be a great time to show it, just a lil bit. "Do you think you can guess the exit to take you home?", I said. One of them thought for a second and said, "I think it's this one", and pointed to the very next exit.

I am not in the right lane, and I need to get off, and it wasn't the safest multi-lane merge, but we made it. As soon as I got off at the exit, the phone rang. Is it mine? No, it's Tio's phone. He answered it and handed me the phone; on the other end was a concerned nephew. "Aye fool, I'm looking at the map and my Tio was supposed to be dropped off first, and I don't know what you're trying to pull but we can see the map". Just as I tried to explain my case, the call dropped.

(Aye, God?!?!?) So now I must ask Tio, "Do you know how to get to where you live?", to which gramps responded with a hearty laugh followed by, "no hablo ingles". Of course. He gave the exact response he was supposed to give because I'm pretty sure God doesn't love me right now.

Just then I hear the teens start to bicker back and forth about something. "You all OK back there? Are we going in the right direction?", I ask. Tio's phone rang again and my phone pops on at the same time, but it's not functional. Tio answers and the nephew wants to talk to me again. "Aye fool, you hung up on me and you're still not going the right way", he said, "look, my phone froze and it's not turning back on", I pleaded, "that's not my problem. You're supposed to have that information", he said, then the call drops again, and my stomach did, too. Crowning.

The teens have reached an agreement, "hey sir, it's coming up on the next street", the girl says. We're less than a block from the next street, so to make sure I ask them, "At the light?" For somebody so sure, she shrugged again. I could've taken a bite out of the steering wheel; I was so angry. So, I say again, "I don't want to pass it up so if you can let me know, that'd help me out a lot". They look at each other. I'm baffled.

28

I have gramps call his nephew again, just to show some good will, and the call goes right to voicemail. In my head he's mounting up the troops to come get his Tio from certain danger.

I don't go to church as much as I used to, but sometimes when I'm in trouble I tend to sing gospel songs. I whispered to myself, "And I know it was the blood, OH YES", and I can almost hear God saying "Nope! Don't try to talk to me now.". Then one of the teens pointed without saying anything, I just happened to see it in the rear view. I said to the teens in a masked, urgently annoyed tone, "this street?", and the boy nudged the girl, "say something!", and she said in the softest voice imaginable, "yes, sir". I made a right turn and my phone turned on again and now it's functioning!

There were about three more blocks before the sweet, innocent, whisper-teens were dropped off. How we got there, I will never know, but they got out without saying goodbye, which was more than fine with me. Perhaps they were scared but dang it that's when you're supposed to be the most vocal, no? I know everybody is built differently but you just need to have some skills if you're going to be in the big cruel world. I digress.

Now it's time to get Tio home since my GPS is back working. I got a call coming in and it was the nephew, but the signal was terrible, and the call ended up dropping, yet again. I called right back, and he answered, "don't worry about it, we're already on our way", and he just hangs up. CROWNING!

And that's not all, because as soon as he hung up, just as we're merging onto the freeway, Uncle Modelo threw up on me, himself and my door. TAH DAH! What was once a faint stench of Corona-smelling burp air, is now A FULLY REALIZED, stomach lining-traveled beer aroma.

The old man now feels the need to apologize so he keeps trying to shake my hand. I'm trying to drive and push him off at the same time. He took his puke-dampened hands and touched my hand several times on the 12-minute trip to his location. Can I punch this dude? Is he past the age where I can punch him, just to get him to stop touching me? There's no way to explain that. Especially not when the cavalry is on their way to rescue their kidnapped Uncle from the evil Uber driver.

"One day when I was lost, he diiiied up on the cross...", I sang softly. Is there a way that I could just drop him off at McDonalds and be forgiven, just so I'm no longer being tracked on the app? I'm sure he'd sober up, and the cops could take care of him. Yeah, I'd face some backlash but the explanation about my fear of an imminent collision with his family could get me out of that, couldn't it? I just wanted this to be over. I should stop driving.

When we stopped, he was still trying to apologize and shake my hand. I'm just trying to leave before his cavalcade of nephews pull up. I finally convinced him to get out just as the front door was opening. I waved goodbye and I Prius-peeled off only to look down and see that he had left his wallet. Welp, too bad, because if you think I'm going back after I just escaped certain mob action, you're on coke! Just before I turned to get onto the highway, I had a change of heart, and I made a U-turn.

I went back to his house - I did not get out. I made another U-turn as I pulled up to the house and I Frisbee-chucked that wallet out of my passenger side window, and it hit the steel screen door, and it fell onto the first step. So, with all four windows rolled down to soften the stench of Modelo puke, I pulled off. But I bet I got that $150 throw-up fee from Uncle Tio's nephew, though! And as angry as I was with those teenagers, they low-key saved the day. "And I know it was the blood, foooooor meeeeeeee".

SMALL WORLD

I ran into a woman who was friends with a woman I was in a long-suffering situationship with. Apparently, I had met her before and hadn't remembered as I picked her up from the airport. She kept who she was a secret until I dropped her off, at which time she revealed who she was, where we had met, and she urged me to, "get it together" with her friend. I was both startled and flattered...we never got it together.

One more... while talking to a young white woman passenger from Michigan, I told her that I was from Indiana. "I am too", she said. "Really? I'm from Hammond but I was born in Michigan City, Indiana". "Me too!", she said in laughy, disbelief. "Were you born in Memorial or St. Anthony's?", I said and she said, "St. Anthony's!". "OH SHOOT, ME TOO!", I said, and we both laughed, overjoyed by the random discovery.

I made one last half-serious joke, "Now if you tell me you were born in November, then I'll pull this Prius over right here", her face dropped and I said, "GET THE EFF OUTTA HERE!". "OH MY GOD, YES I WAS!", and we laughed for another few seconds. At this point I was scared to clarify any further. Turns out we were the same age, born in the hospital just days apart. You never know.

Chapter 6:
Burnt Orange Bodily Fluid

Trigger warning - Gross factor. It's a sunny day and Uber has just changed how their fares are "calculated", again. When we started there was .10 per minute and between .80 to $1.00 per mile, and around this time it switched to some unknown, incalculable, mystery system that basically comes out to between 30-40% of whatever they calculate - a far cry from the 80% we used to get, but I digress.

The reason I bring this up is because this fare was $5.00 and there were three people, and on top of there being three people, a young lady stopped me once I got into the parking lot and asked me to pull into the handicap space because her grandmother has a chair. I had just made a vow that I wasn't going to be lifting wheelchairs in and out of my car anymore. I really feel like there should be a separate vehicle for them. This feels like a lot to do for just five bucks, and I thought about leaving, but then my guilt kicked in, and I thought about my own beautiful mother, so I caved.

I pulled up to the handicap space. By the time I had gotten out, she was helping her grandmother into the car and leaving the chair for me to fold and load, which I did as they all got in the car. The woman in the front seat, the grandmother in the back passenger seat and a young man, about 19 or 20, sitting behind me. Once I get back in the car, it smells like whatever you think it might smell like, based on this sentence.

The smell actually said, "hello David, we're gonna be here for a lil minute", and as soon as I smell it, I get a ping on the app that says they've added a stop. There are few things I hate more than the ol' stop add.

Some people use it to lure you in with the long ride, then change it once they're in to a much shorter ride, and others do the exact opposite... they'll have a short ride, then change it to something ridiculous like Orange County or deep in the valley during rush hour. Anyway, I'm stuck now because I can't ask them to get out. I'm just stuck.

We're on our way to CVS and the car smells like someone has gone a profound number of days in the same clothes and without a shower, whilst doing everything one would do during those days. Once we get to CVS and the young lady gets out, the smell doesn't leave. I can count the granddaughter out, and all I could feel was sadness. Why would you have your grandmother out here like that? I clocked it when she got in the car... how she was dressed. It just didn't feel like she was put together well.

The granddaughter used the entire five minutes of wait time, then she came out explaining to Granny about what prescription and food she couldn't get, posturing like she was about to go back in, but I assume she felt me waiting to explode had she said she was going back in. Remember, that smell is still lingering like Covid symptoms. Granddaughter gets back in the car, and we have five minutes to the final destination, and though I'm not squeamish, my stomach is starting to ask my brain, "Big dawg, how much longer do we have?".

The windows are down as we cruise at a frantic but controlled 45 in a 35 when Granny moans, "Cara", the granddaughter, "roll that window up". Cara obliges by rolling the window up a little bit. A few seconds later Granny reiterates this desire, "Cara, roll the window up, I'm cold".

Cara proceeds to roll the window up just a bit more. I'm watching Cara's fingers like a hawk. Then finally, in a slightly elevated and annoyed tone, Granny demands again, "CARA, I'M COLD. ROLL THAT WINDOW UP!", and Cara rolled the window all the way up! I couldn't get the words out of my mouth fast enough, "Cara, don't close that window", and this is how I know that Cara knew that her Granny was stankin, because she rolled the windows all the way back down!

We finally pulled up to their apartment, and I got the wheelchair out of the hatchback, they put her in it, and I got back in the car. I felt bad until, the smell said, "Hey Dave", once I got back in the car. I now must cancel my next trip because I can't pick anybody else up with my car smelling like this. I must go back to CVS, go home and get some solution, and prepare to doctor this smell out of my car, for which I'll have to spend a couple of hours that I could've spent making money.

It's 40 minutes later and I got the solution but I'm sitting in the driver's seat when I spray the passenger side, then I spray poor Granny's side and for some reason, something said, "David, spray behind you", and when I got out of the car to look in the back seat, TWO 6-INCH LONG STREAKS OF BURNT ORANGE-COLORED (excuse my language) SHIT STREAKS are on the seat behind me! I'll be damned!

It wasn't Granny. I'm sorry Granny, but y'all knew this boy was stankin before you got in my car. I blame you, too. That boy has been stankin and hasn't changed those damn pajama pants for days, and you would put him in somebody's car like that? No more pajama pants in my car. Nope! The day is over. Somebody's gotta pay me for the money I'll miss for the rest of the day. (they did, by the way. Not enough, but they paid). Follow your first gut. Wash your butt.

Chapter 7:
2AM And She's On Drugs

One night in West Hollywood at around one a.m., I was dropping off two white women in their early twenties. I pulled up to the apartment, and I heard one of the women say goodbye to the other one. I didn't realize this was a two-part trip. Only when I got to the second apartment in Beverly Hills, just a block from Whole Foods, I stopped the car, and I didn't hear the normal movement from a passenger about to get out of the car. I turned to make sure she wasn't sleeping, and she wasn't.

She was looking straight ahead, but she didn't look at me when I turned around. I said, "ok then. Have a great night". The young blond, white girl doesn't budge. She still doesn't look my way; she's just staring off into space. I try again, "hey there. This is it, right?", and she just robotically turns her head toward me. I'm feeling faint because it's something out of Halloween III: Season of the Witch. Is she a robot? Who let a damn robot in my car? I try again, "is everything ok? This is your stop, right?", "I don't know", she said. "Where is your apartment?", I asked. "It's wherever you left me", she said, ghostfully. It's late, she's white and young, she's zonked out of her mind and I am terrified.

I'm baffled and it feels like the clock is ticking. It's almost 1:30 a.m. by this time. How long before she either calls for the police or before I'm pulled over by the police and the tears start flowing and the cops start cuffing. I don't know what to say or how to help. I can recognize a drunk person, but she wasn't that. She wasn't slurring her words, no weird movements, none of that. She was just zonked out. Is this a drug, is this a condition, is this how it ends?

"Hey, I don't know what that means", I said. "Well, I don't know what you want me to say", she said. "Ma'am, I'm trying to get you home.", I said. "Well do that", she says back to me. "Where do you live?", I ask, again. "I'm where you left me", she rebuts. I turn around, and I take a deep breath. I call the number attached to the account, just in case it wasn't hers and thank God, it's ringing. The relief was short-lived because two seconds later I heard her phone ringing. OH, MY GOD, this is her trip! I'm calling her phone! (LOL)

Hey, God. You there? Like, for real. It's your boy! I went on live, national TV and shouted you out, remember? (It was back in 2006.) After my quick prayer to God, I tried another approach. "Is there anywhere that you would like to go?", I ask. I thought that this was sweet enough of a question to turn the tides, change the trajectory of the moment.

This was years before, but I felt like I was trying to pick the perfect Chat GBT prompt. Maybe it can jog her memory on what do to or where to go. "I just wish you stopped yelling at me!", she exclaimed in a raised, crackling voice. Lord, this is a horror movie! I swear, she looked just like MEGAN from the movie, only this was before MEGAN. There's a thing that black men know in this country - DO NOT MAKE A WHITE WOMAN CRY! If you do, your butt is TOAST and she's almost there, I'm almost toast. They JUST put me at the bottom of the stove and the clock is ticking.

Just then like manna from heaven her phone rang, and she answered it. "I don't know.

I just know he keeps asking me the same question (her voice cry-cracks) and he keeps yelling at me", she said. Everything in me wanted to yell out "Ain't nobody yelled at you!", but that would for sure accelerate the clock and we don't want that. I assume the person on the other end asked her to pass the phone to me because that's what she did without saying a word. "Oh my God, I am soooo sorry. Can you drop her back off where you picked her up?", said the person on the phone. "Yep! On my way right now!" I handed the phone back to NaNu NaNu and I drove as pleasantly as I could back to the Troubadour, a famous concert venue in West Hollywood, which is where I picked them up.

As soon as I pulled up, there were three women ready to accept her. They helped her out of the car and one of them said to me, "I'm so sorry about that", and they stumbled off. I'm going to bed. I'm about to stop driving at night. I'm about to stop driving period. What the heck word was that? Gospel music on the drive home.

What I've learned.

I have the power to set the tone in the car. Often people just want to catch the ride and aren't aware or don't care about whether I have a place to wait for them. Some people are on a really busy street and as they're taking their sweet time either coming out to the car, the last 12 cars that have passed me have either angrily laid on their horn or have come within inches of swiping my car and it's stressful. It's stressful because it's dangerous.

Also, if my car is hit and depending on how long the car might be in the shop, I may not have the cash to sustain myself until it's fixed. By the time the passenger has gotten into my car, I'm in a mood and who knows what the passengers have been through this morning, and it creates a tension-filled space that we have to share. Then when I'm mature enough, I swallow my pride, take a deep breath and I ask, "how is your morning?", and almost every time, it immediately releases the tension out of the car like a deflated balloon.

Even if we don't end up having a conversation, I've just reset the tone. It's happened so many times and while some people are completely inconsiderate, a lot of people just aren't aware. I've had so many great conversations that almost didn't happen, all because of the way the ride started, because I wasn't mature enough to clock what was going on.

People would rather trade time for control. After so many trips you learn that the GPS knows best 97% of the time. People somehow think they all have a quicker route and that is very rare.

But people don't care that the new route is clearly taking us longer, they just want to feel that it was because of them that we got there, and the time doesn't matter as much. Better said, if they're going to be late, they'd rather risk it being because of their route rather than a driver's GPS (which is identical to theirs).

Most people can't wait to open up. I start each ride the same way. I make sure I have the right name and when they get in the car I say, "how's the day?". If they're curt and don't feel like talking, then it's a silent ride, which is fine by me because 99% of the time I'm listening to a podcast in my left ear. If they seem like they're up to it, then they'll make a comment about the weather, traffic or how their morning is going, then we have ourselves a conversation.

I've heard the most salacious stories you'd ever want to hear and it's mainly because they'll never see me again and I'm a willing ear. At the end of the day people just want to be heard, across the board. You'd be surprised what you can get out of them if you just listen.

Passengers are fascinating. I always ask married couples their advice. I always tell Australian people about the "Drop Bears" prank that one Australian couple played on me, never fixing it so I had to wait weeks to find out the truth from another Australian couple. People from northern California have a different texture than southern CA. Northern CA people, especially from "The Bay", I can always tell. It feels like they've interacted more with diverse crowds than people from LA. They have a similar texture to places like the Midwest, where I'm from, or the south where I went to college. (TSU - GO BIG BLUE)

People with different political views are people too. People don't know that they're a type. I see them coming a mile away. I can tell when someone is about to slip into a political view by the questions they're about to ask and it's the same whether it's an eighty-year-old Persian woman, a sixty-year-old White woman from Beverly Hills, or forty-year-old man from Arizona. There are always a few tester comments to see if I'm accepting to whatever thinly veiled, borderline problematic thing they're about to say.

But before they open their mouths about politics, I've learned that we have the greatest conversations. There's a great sketch on SNL called Black Jeopardy and it features Tom Hanks who plays a right-wing good ole boy from the south. In this sketch the black people and Tom Hanks' character find out they have more in common than they ever would've thought, and it's so true.

I've had the most enlightening and wonderful conversations with some people who believe much differently than I do, but somehow that damn party line keeps getting in our way. Don't get me wrong... some things I have a HARD line on, but before those things are revealed and sometimes, they never are, people are just people trying to figure it out.

Chapter 8:
Celebrities

Look, I know what you're here for, you're here for the celebs. You want to hear just how many I've driven around, what they said, who they were with and if they were mean, right? I know, but those are stories that I will get to. I don't want to ruin all the suspense that I didn't already ruin in the marketing. (LOL) In the meantime, I've met Julia Robers on a delivery. She held the door open for me and grinned when she noticed me noticing her. I kept it together though.

There was a brief Bobby Monaghan from SNL ride to the Grove. While dropping off another passenger, I ran into/re-met another SNL alum, Kyle Mooney. I say re-met because we were in a short film together, YEARS ago (Shout out Crooks and PP). He definitely did not remember me but he's super nice and one of the funniest people alive.

David Arquette made me wait about 10 minutes and then he tipped me $20 cash once the ride was over, he was a nice guy. There was Matt Lucas from Bridesmaids, Wonka and Gladiator2, cool dude and he also gave me a great tip. There was also Tommy Chong and his wife. I remember Stevie Wonder's "Superstition" was playing and he loved it! I try not to show them that I know who they are under certain circumstances; I just give a smile and a polite nod, and he caught it.

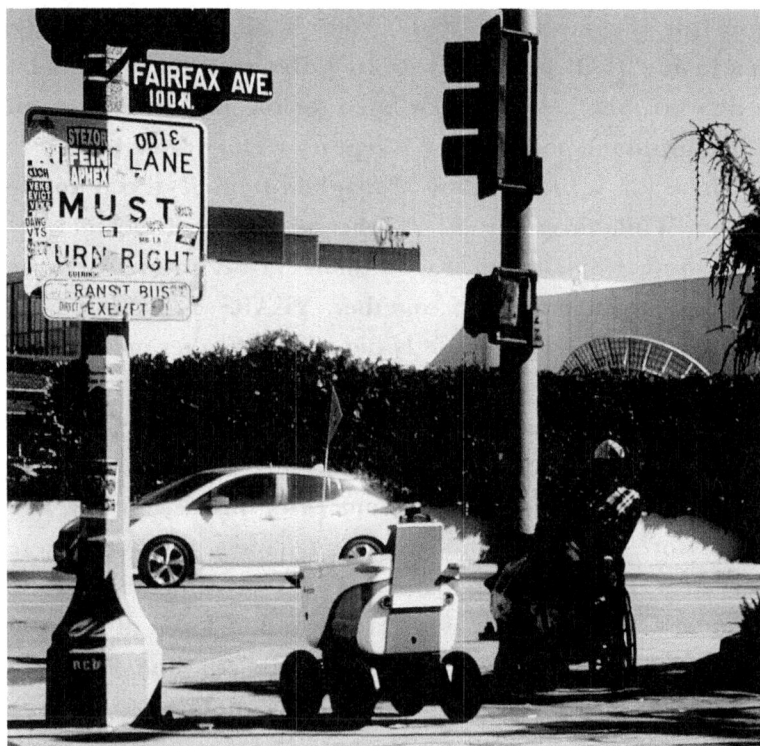

He complimented me on my music choices (This was on my personal playlist), gave me a wink and a nod then they left. I gave a ride to Kelly McCreary, who portrays Dr. Maggie Pierce on Grey's Anatomy. It was dark and I suspected the last thing a woman wanted to hear from a stranger at night was how he recognized her, so I waited until she was getting out of the car to say, "You are my girlfriend's favorite character on the show", and it seemed to have taken her by surprise but she was very delighted and thanked me for saying so.

I've also driven around several influencers, musicians (Jidenna before he was a "Classic Man", dressed to a T, even back then) and the drummer for Death Cab for Cutie (we had an amazing conversation about politics), that made me start listening to their music. (I Will Possess Your Heart) is my joint!!! I've had reality show stars from Big Brother to Real Housewives of (several cities, including ATL), that have all been driven around by yours truly! Anything can happen in LA. Anything!

Chapter 9:
Destiny's Child-ish

One day in West Hollywood, I pulled up to a property and before I knew it, someone was opening the back passenger door. I looked at the name as I always do and didn't think anything of it. Before she got in, I could only see the bottom half of her face. GREAT smile! She greeted me, I replied and we were off.

By now I'm sure you understand that I'm an engager. I'm not pushy, unless you're rude, then I'll talk the entire time. But this day I'm being uncannily pensive plus KJLH, (Stevie Wonder's radio station 92.3), which I usually play when black folk of a certain age and demo get in the car... they were on a run, playing hit after hit. At some point we're both humming along with the songs being played but we're still not saying anything. I heard her singing and I remember thinking, "aawwwww", she's probably out here trying to make it. Good luck because it's tough", says the Uber-driving actor LOL

Hearing her sing, for some reason made me think that I was being rude and I asked, "so, (name on the Uber app) where you from?", I asked. We're now 10-15 minutes into the trip. She answers, "I live in New Orleans". I said, "Oh yeah, my grandfather is from Dubach, LA", she said, "yeah, I know where that is". "Really? Most people from there don't even know", I said. "Yeah, my Mom is from Louisiana, so she knows all that stuff", she replied.

Wait a minute – for some reason song lyrics rushed into my thoughts, "My Daddy Alabama, Mama Louisiana...", and without even seeing her face, I know that Solange Knowles is in the back seat of my car! Even though she's seated far against the door and low so I can't really see her face, I don't want to be a creeper by extending my neck to get a better view of her in the rearview, so instead, I chilled...

What do you say when, 15 minutes into the ride, you discover one of your favorite artists in the backseat of your car. Just think of how weird and discombobulating that sentence sounds – only in LA. I played it cool and just before she got out, I told her my favorite song of hers; "Losing You", and I apologized for not recognizing her right away. She said thank you and was mortified that I apologized for not recognizing her. "KJLH was Jammin, wasn't it!?", she said. And just like that she was gone, just like Cranes in – my bad, I had to do it.

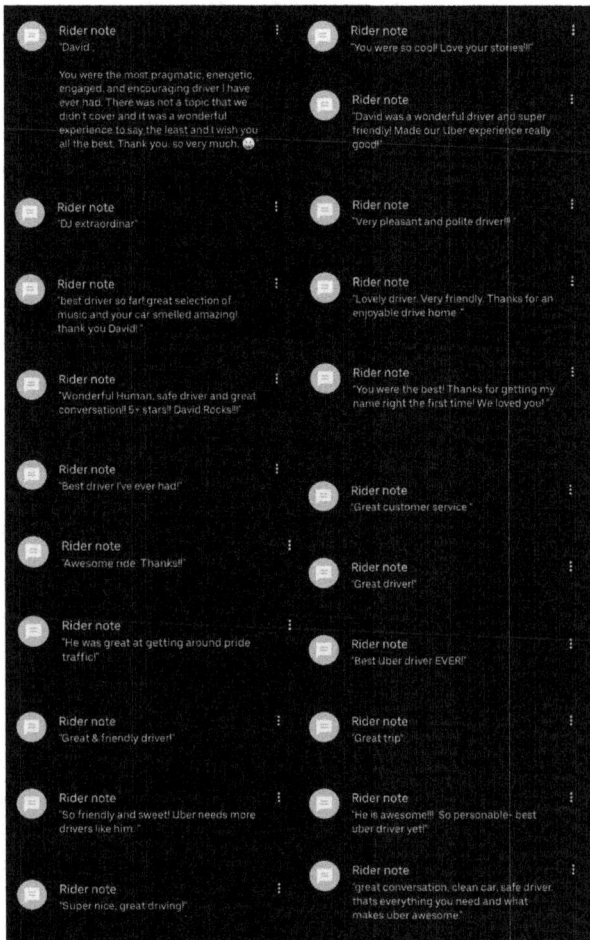

Rider note
"David ;

You were the most pragmatic, energetic, engaged, and encouraging driver I have ever had. There was not a topic that we didn't cover and it was a wonderful experience to say the least and I wish you all the best. Thank you, so very much. 😊

Rider note
"DJ extraordinar"

Rider note
"best driver so far! great selection of music and your car smelled amazing! thank you David! "

Rider note
"Wonderful Human, safe driver and great conversation!! 5+ stars!! David Rocks!!"

Rider note
"Best driver I've ever had!"

Rider note
"Awesome ride. Thanks!!"

Rider note
"He was great at getting around pride traffic!"

Rider note
"Great & friendly driver!"

Rider note
"So friendly and sweet! Uber needs more drivers like him. "

Rider note
"Super nice, great driving!"

Rider note
"You were so cool! Love your stories!!"

Rider note
"David was a wonderful driver and super friendly! Made our Uber experience really good!"

Rider note
"Very pleasant and polite driver!! "

Rider note
"Lovely driver. Very friendly. Thanks for an enjoyable drive home "

Rider note
"You were the best! Thanks for getting my name right the first time! We loved you!"

Rider note
"Great customer service "

Rider note
"Great driver!"

Rider note
"Best Uber driver EVER!"

Rider note
"Great trip"

Rider note
"He is awesome!!! So personable- best uber driver yet!"

Rider note
"great conversation, clean car, safe driver. thats everything you need and what makes uber awesome"

NBA ICONS. MUSIC LEGENDS. NAKED LADIES.

At a certain point in the journey Uber got into the delivery business. Now, this was very troubling for me because I have 1500 deliveries with Task Rabbit, who has completely dropped the ball on that portion of the business. From October 2014 until January 2018, I was averaging four or five deliveries per day, at anywhere between $28-34 per delivery. That went away not because the demand went away, but instead because of Task Rabbit's inability to keep marketing the service after IKEA bought part of the company in 2017. I went from three to five deliveries per day to ZERO. That's not a demand thing, that's not an inordinate number of new Taskers flooding the market... that's poor management.

I even had regular customers who stopped booking me all at once, mainly because they could no longer find me on the app/website - but I digress.

I explained all of that for context. The other day I got an offer to deliver something that was going to take 20 minutes, and I was offered $4.57. I turned it down. There have also been times when I get to the pickup location for a passenger fare, and someone will hand me something in the window and I would refuse on the strength of having just made $30 the day before for a similar 10–15-minute trip. No way I was going to now take this envelope across town for eight damn dollars. It was crushing.

These days, depending on the price and location, I'll take it. I love connecting with people but if it allows me drive by myself and play music or podcasts out loud without a passenger, then I'll take it.

There was the time that I had to deliver a full-sized portrait/picture of a topless 60-year-old woman to the topless 60-year-old woman in the picture. And I guess she thought it'd be great to receive this topless painting of her, whilst topless, because she opened the door as free as the day she was born. Topless and 60. It was awkward, but I admired her attitude. She could see that I was blushing about it, and she found that even funnier, so I gave a quick Bobby DeNiro nod, and I said, "Not bad for your 40s". She really ate that up!

There was another time where I had a basket to deliver out near one of the beaches. It's getting dark and the addresses are hard to see, especially the way these houses are configured. As I'm searching for the address. I can see a garage door open and there's a guy with no shirt or shoes on, collecting his Uber Eats.

Then as that garage door was closing, I finally saw the address and I yelled, "EXCUSE ME!", and after a second or two the door stopped then started opening back up. As I carefully approached the garage in my most non-threatening way, damn near with hat in hand, the door opens completely to reveal one of the greatest point guards to ever play in the NBA, (it was 18-year veteran, eight-time all-star, two-time MVP), Steve Nash. "Oh, s**t" slipped out of my mouth before I could even tell him that I had a package for him. (Pause- never mind). I gave him the delivery, told him I was a fan, and I kept it moving. He was cool.

Speaking of basketball, I stopped to get a package from somewhere in LA when immediately I spotted the six-eight-ness of one of my favorite basketball players growing up and that was one Jalen Anthony Rose. Although I've never had a chance to converse, I have met him two other times and all have been gracious. I got the package, and he gave me a pound, and I kept it moving even though there were 148 questions I would have loved to ask him. "GIVE THE PEOPLE WHAT THEY WAAANT" and get Jalen back on ESPN! Also, bring back The Jalen and Jacoby podcast!

Another package, this time labeled with the name of the couple the delivery was for... but in an effort to hurry and get it done, I just wasn't paying enough attention. I pulled into the driveway of a very nice property in the hills of Beverly and as I got out of my car, I was approached by a big Al Borland, Bob Vela, Brawny Paper Towel lookin' dude, wearing a flannel and a gun on his hip. I told him who the package was for, and he took it back to his security booth.

On my way back to my car I could see that two topless vans carrying several passengers had pulled up. These vans are "Hollywood Homes" tour vans. One of them said through a bull horn, "are you here to pick up Justin and Jessica (Timberlake)?", which happened to be the names on the package that I had hardly paid any attention to. And after answering them "no", I remember feeling a bit like a doof for not realizing where the package was going, and then immediately afterward, I remember feeling bad for them.

Although millionaires, I did wonder about how easily accessible someone's HOME was for complete strangers! Three vans full of tourists pulling up to your house where your family lives, that's a creepy life. Oh well, Cry Me A River, eh? I'm sorry, that's the last time...

Chapter 10:
Quinta Brunson

I have met Quinta five times (see, we're on first name basis), all before the juggernaut of a show that is Abbott Elementary (which I can't wait to guest star on). I met her for the first time in Silver Lake, briefly. The second time we were both at the same bar and I told her that we had a friend in common, (Shout out Warren. Another actor/director GO BIG BLUE). The third time I met her I was in Hollywood, where I live, and I was walking from Chipotle. As we approached each other I could tell that she knew we had met but just couldn't place where... that's a common thing in LA.

You greet with, "good to see you", just in case you've met the person. Nothing's worse than, "nice to meet you", followed by, "we've met already", OOPS!"Do I know you?", she asked, "Yeah, we've met before", I said. "Are you going to (famous actor) party?".

There was a watch-party for a famous actress, and it was in my neighborhood. I wasn't invited but I had friends who were. She was unsure about where it was, and I was able to assure her that she was in the right place, because I had a friend who was there. Short, quick, sweet.

The fourth time I met her, we had a very sitcom-like moment, and it was the first time I picked her up as an Uber driver. She was across the street, I was at a long light, she decided to cross the street as my light changed, but I didn't notice. Once I made the left turn, I pulled over and noticed that she had crossed the street. Then I made a U-turn and then a right turn to put me back on the street I was originally on - only to find out that she had crossed the street again.

I was highly perturbed, but I couldn't get mad because I was familiar with her and I thought she was hilarious, so we made the best of it. She's the most pleasant, unassuming person you'd ever meet and I'm sure she's the same now, post Abbott success. Can you tell I'm trying to get a guest star? LOL

The last time I saw her was the second time I was her driver. I don't think she recognized me, but I told her about our previous funny interaction and we talked shop. She was developing a show at the time and there's nothing more that I wanted to hear than someone who was actively acting in, writing on, and developing their own show, it was/is the dream.

She shared some details about the process, we laughed about knowing some of the same people that didn't get paid by a certain network on time, or at all. No mix-up this time, just a great conversation with an already successful star. For real, last season of Abbott is approaching, I need that audition! To my Agent and my Manager, I NEEDS THAT AUDITION!!!

Chapter 11:
Turtle From Entourage

Entourage was the show that helped me after I landed in LA. I got a Netflix account so I could catch up on The Wire, but the second show I got into was Entourage, (followed by Curb). It was amazing to see these spots on TV that I was currently learning about. The whole agent game, contracts, big stars vs little stars, friends who've made it who you still have a connection with, friends who've made it who you don't talk to anymore, the stuff I'm experiencing now after 18 years of being in LA and the entertainment business. So, imagine my surprise when Jerry Ferrara, otherwise known as Turtle, hops in my car for an Uber ride.

When I meet celebs, I try to be the opposite of what they'd expect, (except for the time I met Denzel. That's another book. See my Substack for that one. Sorry D), but I want them to know they're not going to be bothered by me. Jerry (Ferrara) got in the car, and I immediately let him know that I know who he is, just with an, "oh, snap. What's up man. I'm a fan.", then I keep it moving. This was around the time he was playing Proctor on the show Power. I asked him about his experience shooting, "that scene", toward the end of the show. And once the trip was over, we sat and talked basketball for at least five or ten minutes. Cool dude.

The second time Jerry got in my car was less than a month later. This time he was with his someone and they got in the car first and said, "for Jerry?", I remember being annoyed by something that had just happened, so I may have answered in a funky tone.

Thirty seconds later Jerry gets in the car, and we recognize each other at the same time, and we freak completely out, startling the friend. "Oh man, we just, not too long ago, he was my, I gave him a ride", we both said, as the friend tried to figure out what was happening.

After the hubbub, we got on with the trip and I dropped them off in the hills, only to be called before I could even end the trip to turn around and get them because they were at the wrong house. They were both apologetic, but I didn't care because I was in the middle of an Entourage episode. I was Turtle in this situation! We got to the next house, and I dropped them off, again... this time I ended the trip.

The phone rang and they were at the wrong house, again. This time they were very, very apologetic. They swore that they had it right this time, as they tried not to place blame. We laughed off whatever embarrassment was there, and we drove the four to five minutes to the next and hopefully final location. We get there, I drop them off and I'm out. You guessed it, IT WAS THE WRONG HOUSE AGAIN!

Now I'm feeling like Johnny Drama without the MOTW money. The next house was the right one and all was well. I met a person I was a fan of, we had an adventure, and he gave me a great tip!

Chapter 12:
The Lucas Brothers

If you don't know them, they're Black comedians who are identical twins. Along with being on every late-night show performing together, they've also had a cartoon called "Lucas Bros. Moving Company", as well as having written an Academy Award winning movie; a Drama about Fred Hampton's assassination called, "Judas and the Black Messiah". (Daniel Kaluuya won Best Actor for this film)

The first time they got into my Prius they were with another person, and they were all philosophizing about government, trade, and America's foreign policies. It was really inciteful. I mean, I call myself somewhat in the know about news items on any given day, but they were into some other stuff, and I won't share what the final takeaway was, but it was sobering.

The second time I picked them up they were with a different guy; it was from the same location and this time the conversation was right up my Alley. WRESTLING! And not the current WWE nonsense but WWF, the '80s wrestling that I grew up on. Normally I don't butt into conversations unless I'm really excited to talk about it, and most people don't mind. This day I wouldn't have cared because they were talking about the Ultimate Warrior, and I loved the Ultimate Warrior! I talked about one of the first times that I was torn as a kid when both of my favorites, The Ultimate Warrior and Hulk Hogan, squared off at Wrestle Mania VI!

I shared how he was my second favorite, and we went over many of the wrestlers of that time, from Jake the Snake Roberts and Hacksaw Jim Dugan to Coco Beware and Macho Man Randy Savage. The conversation came back to Ultimate Warrior, and one of them said, (and the other two guys agreed), something that my retroactive 10-year-old heart couldn't take. 59

It went, and I quote, "well the Ultimate Warrior was a terrible wrestler". HUH? Whatever do you mean, funny men? How was this a thing that supposedly everybody knows except for me? Something that younger identical twins plus a random white hanger-on can confidently affirm! Better yet, what smarmy, smug, jerk children are assessing how well the Ultimate Warrior is jumping off the top rope and clotheslining the Big Boss Man? Who's paying attention to technique at that age? And if you weren't of age during that time, then who are you to come and tell me that Milli-Vanilli was lip syncing 30 years later?!?

The ride was over for me. I couldn't wait to get these wet blankets out of my car. The worst thing is when you can't wait to talk to yourself after passengers get out of your car because of what they just said or what just happened.I was so angry that I nice-tweeted them about it later and one of them replied, kindly. Do yourself a favor and shut up when it comes to wrestling. Don't ever tell someone that piece of information if they don't already notice it. Hell, I still can't tell the difference. RIP Warrior.

QUESTIONS:

The mini stories will now consist of the top questions from passengers and friends.

HOW MUCH LONGER WILL YOU DRIVE?

Hell, hopefully by the time you read this I will have retired already. Truth is I'm tired (sorry, I had to). I've tried a few things that I thought would carry me away from the car but either they didn't pan out, or I didn't stick with them long enough to see them pan out. Honestly, when I think about when I started, I never, ever thought I'd still be driving. I just knew I would have been on season five of a great TV show by now; and quite frankly I didn't plan well.

I have a couple of ideas that I'm locked in on now, they're just going to take some time. Put it like this, come check my Instagram a year from the book's release, and I bet you $5 that I won't be driving anymore, at least not for money. BET! Seriously, I'm almost done. BURNT ORANGE let me know that my days were super numbered!

61

Chapter 13:
The Car Chase Through Koreatown

Back when I was still driving at night, I stopped at a restaurant in Koreatown to grab a Coke to keep me up and to rest because I had been out for quite a while. I hate it when people park over the lines. Close to the line isn't ideal either but it's better than across the line. This day I was the culprit unknowingly.

As I'm sitting in my car, an Asian man pulls up on my passenger side. He gets out and goes straight into the restaurant and stays for a while. When he came back outside, and just as he opened his door to his car he yelled, "learn how to f***king park you motherf***er. Can't drive!", right into my partially rolled-down passenger side window, and at me. Before he could hop right into his RAV4, I fired a few expletives back at him! It came out of nowhere. If he had told me that I was parked wrong, then I could've fixed it before he came back out, and everything would be all good.

I didn't feel comfortable anymore, so I left as he waited in the car for who knows what. When I pulled out of the parking lot, I got stopped by a light just outside the restaurant and he pulled up beside me and he was still talking crazy, screaming at me from his car. I fired back yet again and I unkindly ordered him to leave me alone and just drive, and I drove off as the light turned green. When I turned and reached yet another light, he was still talking, so at this point I already know what I'm going to do and I'm not proud of it... I'm not entirely ashamed either. Let me preface this with this – I should not have let this man take me out of my character.

63

I had a large Coke (or Pepsi) from the restaurant, and it was more than halfway full, and I prepared to make a left just as the traffic reached the light, but first, I would throw this heavy, half-full cup of carbonated beverage at his RAV4 and flee. Since I didn't have a sunroof, I would have to get creative and treat it like a quarterback flicking to the fullback on an option play.

BOOF! The drink hit the back rear driver's side of his RAV4 and I skirted off into the night down this side street - only this guy must've been an F1 driver, because I made SURE there was no room for him to turn and follow, due to the heavy oncoming traffic that I narrowly escaped, myself. Nope, that man made this impossible left turn and was ON. MY. ASS! The chase was on in the mean streets of Koreatown.

I darted down a street; he darted down the street. He tailed me in his RAV4 with a furious, rage-filled fervor. I'm running stop signs; he's running stop signs because it doesn't matter to him! This is my third car chase, but it has been years since the last one, so I'm exhilarated but I'm also terrified. If THIS guy would chase ME through the streets, (and I should've thought about this beforehand), then what the hell does he have, because he cannot justify this chase on the confidence of his fight game. There's no way! Now my stomach hurts just a little bit because I'm nervous. Damn. I hit another side street; he hit the same side street; I bend the corner; he follows damn near on two wheels around that same corner! I've got a plan.

I'm on another side street and I'm going to gain speed on the straightaway then dart down one of the streets and I'll have to get a bit reckless as I lose him for good! I'm gaining speed and I'm looking down at each street. Not that one, not that one, not… wait, yeah, this is the one!

I've been gaining speed and now I have a pretty decent lead on him, so I tap the break just enough that I don't roll my car into somebody's front yard, I make a left turn and, if I may borrow some old slang from Chicago, "I got LITTLE", meaning I'm OUTTA THERE!

Remember in The Godfather when Tessio realizes that the jig is up as they start to surround him? That perfectly describes my face when I realized that I passed up ALL those side streets to end up turning down the only dead-end, cul-de-sac street in the bunch. By the time I fully realized, I was three quarters of the way down and my stomach is, yet again, champagne bubbly. I get to the end, and I know that at the very least I need to be facing him by the time the car gets to me, but the cul-de-sac isn't big enough, so I must make a three-point turn, really fast. Once I do, I'm staring down this speeding RAV4, coming at me like John Snow staring down the calvary at the Battle of the Bastards. So, it ends like this, eh? Two tears in a bucket!

He finally reached me and oddly enough he doesn't try to box me in. Instinctively I opened the car door and put a foot out onto the ground, and thankfully he does the same, and as soon as his foot touched the ground, I never took the car out of drive, so I pulled my foot back into the car and I peeled off. He still must make a three-point turn before he can follow me and I'm at the corner by the time he even turns around.

I bang a left once I'm at the end of the block and I see a lone car, a Domino's pizza delivery truck about four to five blocks down. That's my target, if I can reach him, bust a right, I can blow this popsicle stand for good!

I'm gaining speed and about halfway through, I can see Ol Ravy back there still at it, with the anger of a man who's been freshly juked. I'm gaining on my target, running stop signs, reckless but focused. I reach the Domino's guy, and I pass him. I then make a sharp right with just enough space as not to have cut them completely off.

It's a wrap now, I'm like Jordan in the GOAT debate, I can't be caught. I'm doing the Deion Sanders dance, but in a car. I saw him one more time after I turned that corner, then I went bye-bye. I made it to Sixth Street, still paranoid, but I was on the way home. PHEW! Do better, David!

WHAT WAS YOUR SCARIEST RIDE?

Along with the one I mentioned earlier in the book, this one lasted almost 40 minutes and psychologically it was just a lot. One day in Echo Park I pulled up to a sort of dead-end street, sort of up a hill. Like I said before, if I don't know exactly where you're coming from, I like to get a vantage point just in case there are four or five of you. That way I can just pull off and leave.

That was tough to do in this instance because of the way this street worked, and I just had to leave it up to chance. Now, it's one of those spicy LA days that happened in late October or early November and it's 90 degrees. My back door opens, and a white man gets in. He's dressed in all black, wearing a black hoodie over a black ski mask and holding a black backpack. My internal gospel song starts to play again, "He never said a mumbling word, OH YES". I slyly grabbed a folding knife that I kept in the car and kept it close as I greeted him. He greeted me back in the most normal way. He didn't take the mask off.

Neither of us tried to make conversation during the ride, and the whole way there I'm wondering about all the scenarios; he can't be about to shoot me, can he?

He can't shoot me if he's on his way to do the shooting. I've never heard of them shooting the Uber driver and then doing the mass shooting. I'm rationalizing at this point. Is he using me to get to the place where he plans to unload on a crowd of people? If so, do I preemptively crash my own car to save people from it? It might sound crazy to you now, but I'm telling you it was 90 degrees, and he was dressed in all black, with a hoodie and a ski mask, what else was I supposed to think?

The final destination (ha) was at a Beverly Hills restaurant, just as swanky as it wanted to be. I pulled up to the place, he got out and said, "thanks", and he just threw his backpack over his shoulder and walked into the restaurant. forty minutes of vigilance, waiting for a weird move, looking for a reason to take action – And of course your brain gets creative and thinks every move is thee move. Man, that trip was a trip.

Chapter 14:
Trapped In A Fancy Hotel Room

This next delivery was different. I got a call from a guy who had left his backpack at The Montage (currently The Maybourne), a fancy Beverly Hills hotel, and he needed it brought to him at one of the beach cities, where he had an "important meeting". This sounded sketchy to me, so I started to decline it, but it was going to help me make my day early, and again I cherish being able to make money and drive without passengers.

The directions were that I'd meet a lady in the lobby named Jewel, but it could only be her, and that I'd have to walk away from the lobby and Jewel would bring me the card key. I remember thinking "why is this so secretive", and "damn I shouldn't have taken this". It feels weird but let's get this day over with Dave, power through."

I go to the hotel, and I ask for Jewel, but they act like they don't know who I'm talking about. One thing about being in Beverly Hills is that LA is already the most, "are you supposed to be here" place in the world, so to now be in Beverly Hills and to be dressed like a courier and to be in a swanky hotel, you stick out like a courier in a swanky hotel. After a few minutes, Jewel walked from out of the back, saw me sticking out and she waved me over. "You Jewel?", I said. "You David?", she said. "yep", I said, and she directed me over to a waiting area away from the lobby. I sat there and waited until she brought me the key. Even when she gave it to me, she walked past me and slid it next to me. What kind of Dave Bond stuff am I involved in right now?

I went up to the room, and I got the laptop and the folders, and I stuck them in the backpack. There was clearly a great time that was had the night before. There were condoms, liquor and there was a tad bit of sugar left on the nightstand, which was weird because why would lines of sugar just be out on the nightstand?

Suddenly I hear talking outside the door as I'm about to exit. I looked through the peephole, and I KNEW IT, two husky dudes with trench coats standing outside the door. One of them knocks on the door and I start sizing up their fire escape game. I'll jump smooove out this window, like on some '90s Wesley Snipes, Jason Borne type shit. (Peep my inclusion skills)

Should I hide? In the closet, under the bed... why do people hide under beds anyway? As I'm trying to find an appropriate place to hide, this John Belushi lookin' dude starts jiggling the door handle. Now I feel stomach thunder again.

"Melodies from heaven. Rain down on me, Rain doooown on maaay. Take me in your arms and hold me close. Rain down on maay.". Surely singing gospel will unlock a certain amount of God-Help because MAN! John stops jiggling the door and the two men in trench coats walk away from the door but that could be a set-up. I'm not dumb! I would walk away from the door too if I'm trying to get you out. That's, "wait for somebody outside a hotel room", 101!

I'm confused, should I be calling the police, or that dude or what? I just want to go home at this point and not even to my LA apartment but back to INDIANA! I want my Mama! (LOVE YOU, MA!) Finally, after about 10-12 minutes, I think the coast is clear and I'm ready to walk out.

My courage is up, I'm ready for anything and quite honestly them walking away from the door actually did work, but I will hit somebody with this Mac book if need be. I cracked the door to see if they would start rushing back to the door and I don't see anything. I clocked where both the stairs and the elevator are, so that I have options. Dave Borne-Bond in full effect. For some dumb reason I've still got the goods with me.

I opened the door all the way and boom, just to the left of me are John Belushi and his boy, and they're looking directly at me. I hit it head-on though, "Y'all need something?", I said. John looked at his guy like, "who is he talking to?". "Had the wrong room number, sorry about that", he said. Mind you, I never stopped walking so he's finishing his sentence talking to my back. I'm heading toward the exit.

Here I am thinking in my Kevin Hart voice, "IT'S ABOUT TO GO DOWN", and the trench coats weren't even for me. I returned the stuff to the dude 45 minutes later and I never saw him, Jewel, Belushi or his friend, ever again. Your mind can have you on some BS missions. I guess that sense of fear is what kept us alive in the stone ages, but I'll be damned if it doesn't have you on some movie-brain stuff. I'm still shocked at how quickly I thought about the window as an escape option.

YOU EVER PUT SOMEONE OUT?

Yes. It doesn't happen often, but I have. As I said earlier when I first started, I was painfully affable but once I found out I didn't have to be extra, things got different. If you respect the fact that it's my car, we'll be fine. We can disagree but I can't have you disrespecting or berating me. Usually, it's because they keep going. You can't be behind me being tough or rude. That's a vulnerable place for me in a crazy world. I like to give a warning; "Is this going to be a problem?" or "can we finish with the trip or do you want to end it here". That's when they sober up and realize the possibilities, and a few times they just chose to keep going, so I ended the trip.

Once a woman got in the car and sat directly behind me and I just can't have that happen. Every time it does happen, I politely say, with the same cadence, "hey, can you do me a favor and sit on this side for me?", and without a hesitation they move right over. Out of the two percent who push back, I've only had to put one person out because of it. "If you're scared then don't be a driver. I've never heard of that before". Yep, you gotta get another car.

Another time was the day after Nipsey Hussle's murder. I pulled up to the maze that is "Park La Brea", the city, I won't even call it an apartment complex, and there was a man who alerted me that his girlfriend was coming down the stairs, then he said, "No rap". I looked back to see if he was on the phone, "excuse me?", I said. "No rap music", he repeated. I won't lie, this probably wouldn't have gone well even if Nipsey hadn't just died, but I was on edge that day.

"Why would you say something like that to me?", I said. "Dude, I'm literally a rapper but I know my girlfriend doesn't like it", he said. By this time the GF was downstairs, worried about the exchange. It was too late. "Y'all got to find another ride to the airport". He didn't even get her bags, she had to bring her own luggage down the stairs, dweeb.

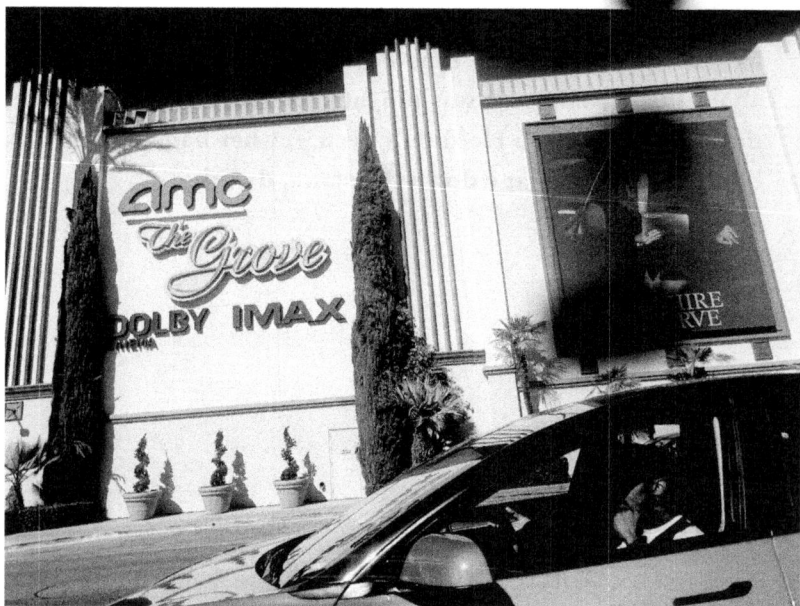

Chapter 15:
Whose Kids Are These?

I want kids of my own. Sometimes I get the chance to play grown-up and hold a kid's hand across a street or let a child know that they might not be doing the right thing at this moment. It gives me a little bit of practice. I can sense you parents judging me, just let me have this one.

One time in Hollywood, I had started early, and I pulled up to an apartment in Hollywood and a man rushed out with his kids in tow. He put them in the car first then closed the door. I know he's not about to ask me to take these kids without him. He then went on to explain that he had an audition and that he had to get to work directly afterward and that he needed me to drop his kids, (daughter 9, son 5), off to two separate schools. Bro. In hindsight I should have said, "NO". I won't lie; I judged him a bit, but the fact remained that time was running, and those kids needed to be at school on time.

I would be doing him a real solid. I'm an actor and I've had the audition/work combo plenty of times. Was I condoning reckless behavior? I'm a complete and total stranger. I mean, had I pulled up with wild hair looking disheveled and distressed, I'd like to think that he would've passed and called another Uber. Perhaps this is just my justification for agreeing to something that was, in all honesty, reckless.

Dave Chappelle once told a story about doing a show for drug dealers who had to pay him a large amount of money in cash. He stuck the 20k in his backpack and proceeded to walk through the streets of New York to the subway. He talked about how terrified he was and how he now had at least a clue as to how it must feel being in possession of something that everybody wants.

His comparison was to women, but I also felt this deep sense of dread and responsibility for having someone else's children in my possession, a complete stranger.

I remember a couple of summers ago, some family gathered for a homegoing service for my Aunt Gladys, (zippa dee doo daah. Love you, Aunt Gladys), and my cousin, who I affectionately call my sister, was in attendance with her family. She and her husband have five kids, and they all call me "Uncle David".

I needed to make a run to the store and the three oldest asked if they could come with me. This was it! This would be my first excursion with these kids. I couldn't wait to not drive until they were all buckled in, and I was fully prepared to yell at a wayward, traffic-bound kid. We stopped at two different places, and it was one of those moments for me that I had missed with my other nieces and nephews. But there wasn't any fear there. Sure, there was a healthy amount of "get these kids home safe", but it wasn't fear. With this stranger's children I felt fear.

Here we are with these kids trapped in the car with a total stranger. I must say that they handled it with the maturity of kids who had gone through this before. The older one was vocal on where to go for the drop-off. I could sense an uneasiness with the whole situation, like she knew it was wrong but here we are so let's just get It over with. I dropped off the 5-year-old first, then the other dread kicked in.

I'm alone with this 9-year-old girl who I don't know, in my car. With all that has happened to children and little girls especially, the pressure to assure her without words that everything was fine, was immense.

Again, I've babysat two-year-olds with diarrhea, I've Heimlich maneuvered a four-year-old choking on a piece of candy (that one was pretty scary), I've taken carloads of kids to the store but for some reason this one felt heavier. I just couldn't believe that this father had left his little kids with me. It just felt wrong - Again, I probably should've rejected the ride. We got to her school, and she told me where to go, she said thank you, then she got out and ran into the school. PHEW! I guess if it had to happen, I'm glad it was me.

WHAT WAS YOUR LONGEST RIDE?

This one is sort of a tie. In Los Angeles on Halloween, West Hollywood blocks off Santa Monica Blvd from La Cienega to Doheny which is about a mile long, and there's a non-stop party packed with the wildest costumes and behavior you'll ever see. It's quite the time. Anyway, if you're a driver then you know to steer clear of that area because it's a traffic nightmare. I got caught in this nightmare on my first day of driving. I picked up a young lady in North Hollywood. She was all dressed up and she wanted to join the festivities. I didn't know what was ahead of me. She was in my car for about two and a half hours. Here I am stuck on Fountain, sort of a cut-through street from West Hollywood to Silver Lake, and she's had enough. She apologizes and she gets out of the car to walk the rest of the way, leaving me in the traffic. I was mad. It took me another hour to get home and ever since that day, I don't even drive that way on Halloween.

The other trip was with a guy who wanted to go to Orange County, and this is back when the fare was worth it to go. This was also before I was jaded and when I was still willing to make trips to places like Huntington Beach, Long Beach, etc. Mid trip he realized that he didn't have to stay, and he asked me if I wanted to make a little more money by waiting for him for a few minutes then take the trip back to LA. The truth is that I was going to have to go back anyway. Sometimes I like to eat at a new restaurant just to give the traffic the chance to die down before I leave. But on this day, I decided I'd take the money.

On the way back to LA, there was major traffic on the 5 Freeway, and we were stuck in it. All together that trip took three and a half hours and while this was in the days when we got paid by distance and time, I still don't desire to be in the car with anyone I didn't know for nearly four hours. It was a decent payday, but never again. We were stuck in one place for over an hour. Nope!

Chapter 16:
The Trader Joe's Bowel Misunderstanding

After you've been driving for a while, you start to pick up some of your favorite places to stop and use the restroom. These places can be a particular Starbucks where you know you don't need to buy anything to use their bathroom, it could be a Ralphs or Pavilion's grocery store where you don't even need a code. One of my places is just about any Trader Joe's. The one in Marina Del Rey... the parking lot is almost always crowded, and they only have single occupancy bathrooms. The Trader Joe's across the street from the Grove has a double occupancy bathroom and has since adapted a code, but it's almost always available. The problem with that one is that you almost always need to enter the ticketed parking lot because those parking spaces on 3rd and Fairfax go fast.

The Trader Joe's on 3rd and La Brea is where this "situation" happened. They have two bathrooms, single occupancy, but there's a lot of space outside the bathroom, just in case you must wait. I'm a homer so I usually wait until I'm home for the big finishes. If I can't then I have no problem two-ing it while I'm out... I just prefer to wait. Grow up, judge yourself...

Today my stop at TJ's was a twofer. I needed water and I needed to release the old water. That parking lot is usually crowded, but it was near dusk, (which is important later), and I guess I had just missed the rush, so I was able to find a spot near the front pretty quickly. I entered the store and headed straight toward the bathroom where both all-gender bathrooms were occupied, where two people were waiting in line, one for each door.

79

An employee hurried out of the second door, and he mumbled something. Whatever he mumbled, the guy standing in line understood it and he switched lines just before I could get in line, so he's now in front of me. I asked him what the employee had said, and he acted like he didn't know. Now I'm annoyed because nobody is saying anything. If the restroom is broken then I won't go in, but if it just stinks then I can hold my breath or whatever. I won't be in there long.

I went for it, and I tried the other door and MY GOD!!! I now understood what the scurrying employee was trying to convey with as little embarrassment as possible. It smelled like all hope was gone, forever. Usually, I try to be mature and breathe normally. It's not because I want to smell it but sometimes stuff will stink - but I honestly tried and couldn't. I once heard the late comedian James Hannah come on stage and start his set with, "is there anyone in here with green Timberlands on? Because wherever you are, you've only got six months to live. You had that bathroom smelling like a morgue". Although I laughed uncontrollably back then, there was nothing funny about this present-day smell. I just wanted to pee and leave. And that's what I did.

When I came out of the bathroom there was an older black woman waiting for me to come out. She was considerably shorter than me so I held the door open with my hand high above her head so she didn't have to touch it and could just walk under my arm. For this she was pleasantly surprised and grateful. I'm still holding and when she has passed from under my arm, I let the door go. As the door is closing, I see her face go from a grateful smile to confusion and horror. She's still looking up at me and all I hear as the door is closing on her is, "In Jesus' name!".

This is why I hate single occupancy bathrooms on the road. That lady thinks that I'm the one who stunk up that bathroom. I didn't really have the time to explain and I couldn't scurry since I was holding the door open for the older black lady who now thinks I only have six months to live.

The mission is now to get my water and get out of this Trader Joe's as fast as possible, because I don't have the time to explain to her that there is nothing wrong with my bowels. I rush to get my water which Trader Joe's annoyingly keep behind the registers, so you must pass the registers up and then come back to the register to purchase the water. By the time I come back to the line, she's walking up in the line next to me, but I pretend like I don't see her. Like an angry mother or a superman foe, I can feel the laser beams piercing through my temple. BE STRONG, DAVID. DON'T LOOK AT HER! I don't care what this lady thinks of my bowel health, but it wasn't me and I shouldn't have to explain anything to her.

"Hey there", she said. Darn it, she's talking to me. I act like I don't hear her. She taps me on the shoulder this time. "Hey there", she repeats. Reluctantly I greet her because I don't want to be rude, but I also don't want to talk to her about my gut health. "Hey", I said. "Is this about the bathroom back there, because that wasn't me". "Young man, it's okay", she condescended. I knew it! She thinks that it was me! I shouldn't be ashamed that she thinks that, but it's principalities in this.

You don't just accuse people without knowing. I had to think of something quick, so I said, "hey, I forgot something. Can you please hold my spot for me?", she agreed, and I didn't grab anything else, I darted to the parking lot.

I didn't run but I speed-walked so fast that my hips were sore when I got to the car - only when I got to my car, I could see her walking briskly out of the store and to the parking lot looking from side to side, I'm 912% sure that she was looking for me because she didn't have any groceries in her hands!!! It was dark now and I lowered my seat so that she didn't see me. She ended up about ten feet in front of my car, on the other side of the grocery cart rack. I even took a picture of her, hopefully by the time this comes out I will have found it. It felt like a social horror thriller, and I survived. Nothing is wrong with my bowels, lady. And I couldn't even get my water.

EVER GOT IN AN ACCIDENT?

I'm proud to say that I'm a good driver. I learned when I was nine in the parking lot of what would be my eventual high school (WILDCATS FOREVER), with my Dad and my stepmother. My Mom didn't like it, but I loved it. Then later my Mom taught me and told me about being a defensive driver and while I didn't know exactly what she meant, I soon learned that people just don't pay attention and are sorely inconsiderate when it comes to driving. And you can multiply that by 13 in a city like Los Angeles.

As an Uber driver I've only been rear-ended. And those rear-ends only came after I had already been stopped.

The second time I was rear-ended, I had literally just left my apartment 12 seconds prior and I was at a stop light when BLAM, I got rear-ended yet again. It was hard and my back was already hurting at the time.

I pulled over, still frazzled and not sure what I wanted to do because at this time I could have didn't have my own car and I was renting from Uber, paying upwards of $230 per week and you only had two accidents, your fault or not, before they snatched away your account/car. This time there was no damage but instead I was worried about the damage to my back because it was quite a jolt. I was fine.

You could tell that the guy was a fast talker and was trying to control and rush the situation. I'm certain that he would've given me the wrong information, but I was ready for all of that. I sat and thought about it. Report him and burn one of two (fault or not) times to report an accident, turn it in and risk not being able to get a new car right away, which was a possibility, or you could just let yet another person get away with rear-ending you.

This theme of not being able to do the right thing because I can't afford to take the time away from driving is a very toxic and extremely stressful way to live. I guess it's my punishment for still being here, for not having implemented the necessary steps to step away from driving... a business, a few vending machines, something! Every day I see it as both a blessing to make my own money and have a "flexible schedule", and I also see it as a curse.

The first time it happened was about three months after I started driving. I was at 7th and Alvarado, close to downtown. I had previously been on the 101 headed north and it was a parking lot, so I asked permission to veer off and take the city streets... the passenger agreed.

The streets were going well, and we were at a stop light and then POW, suddenly we're just catapulted in place. It was truly terrifying. Both my passengers and I were rattled. We got out of the car to find the driver, who had been texting with his head down, casually smoking a cigarette, looking down at his phone, never looking up to check on us or anything. This prompted my passenger to scold him with a lesson in civility and "giving a shit", as he put it. The driver who plowed into us just smirked it off, unphased. Surely, he was a tad frazzled, too and that's just how he shows it.

The police got there, and we did the exchange thing. I called my girlfriend at the time because I didn't think I could drive the car. We were swooped up on by a tow truck and a driver fast talking and looking for business, offering to take my car so that I can pay $300 to get it out. I honestly didn't know how to maneuver.

Looking back, I should have gone to the hospital and let the police take the car just to cover myself. These insurance companies do not care about you so it's better to be safe and get yourself checked out, than trying to be tough and have something happen to you later that you waited too long to act on. Instead, my smart self told my insurance company that I was hit during a fare ride, an admission that got me promptly kicked off their roster of insured folk.

Since it was their fault, I just let the insurance companies handle it, even with the person I slid into because it was raining and the crash caused a chain of them, Uber insurance kicked in as well and I was all covered. My car went into the shop and was kept for about three weeks but the only issue with that was I still needed to drive to make money. The car that the insurance company got for me was not a Prius so what's a brother to do?

Well, this brother still drove and for three weeks I told each and every passenger the same thing before the trip started, "Hey, I was in an accident, and this is the replacement car, and I couldn't change it in the app". Even with that explanation to every single passenger, I still got reported thrice times for "not showing up in the car that was on the app". People are snitches.

That whole ordeal was nerve-racking. I kept wondering when the ball was going to drop, but I made it through. I got my baby back for the time being.

I do have a bulge in one of my disks. I wonder how much of it was from sitting in the car for so many hours and at a desk job before that. I wonder how much of it was from being rear-ended. I wonder. I really should find something else to do...soon.

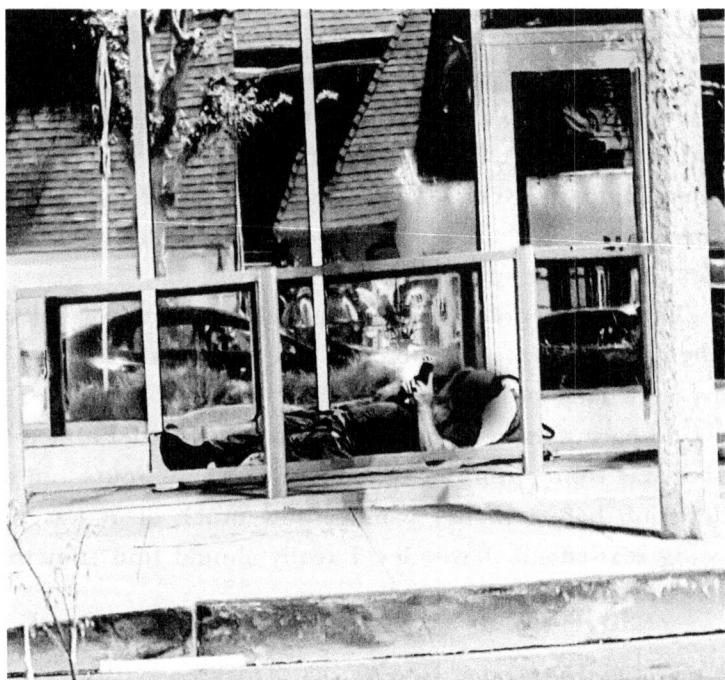

Chapter 17:
I Almost Hit A Kid

In this last story, there was another big family of three in the back seat. This family also didn't speak English. There's a thing that happens when the coast is clear for people to exit a car. Communication breaks down and folks just want to get to where they're going. Often one person will get out and will slam the door on the other person who has scooched over to get out on the same side. Other times both will get out leaving both doors open, thinking that the other person was following behind them.

This time when I dropped the family off, they scurried out in the exact same way, but one of them left the door open for the person who got out on the other side, but the person following them closed it and all was well.

Somehow my number got attached to some property in Nashville, (where I went to college), and for a long time I have been receiving texts and calls from 615 phone numbers asking if I want to sell, so I've grown accustomed to sending them straight to voicemail. Back in the car and my phone starts ringing, I don't recognize the number so I'm doing the same as any other time, only they kept calling and I'm thinking, "they're calling from Texas now, huh?", since most of the calls come from Tennessee are codes.

As I'm on my way to the next ride, I hear, "BOOOO". It came from behind my right elbow and, just as my fingers started to make some kind of eye gouging formation, the phone rang again, and it clicked as I turned around.

The family left this little boy thinking that the other one got him out. The kid was the cutest thing, and he had no earthly idea what my hand was about to do to his face because he scared the hell out of me. He must've realized that he startled me because he kept saying, "boooo", then chuckling afterward. Boo, hell. I answered the phone and though I couldn't understand her words, I understood the frantic tone. I just said, "si mejo, si nino, si, I'll bring him back to you pronto". (Sorry Efrain, I forgot all the Spanish you taught me growing up LOL)

I turned around and dropped him off to the most grateful Mother. Little man was smiling the whole time. He even waved at me on his way out, but I almost elbowed the sh*t out of this little boy.

DO YOU FLIRT WITH PASSENGERS?

Interesting topic. I'm in LA and there is no shortage of amazing women here in this huge city. I won't get too crazy but honestly, everything you want is here in LA. It might be a little fake or superficial, but she's here.

There have been so many women that I would love to have connected with outside of the four doors, but the dynamic is off if you're the driver. Think about it, knowing how creepy some people are, you're picking up women at home or at work. How many guys do you know who can't take no for an answer, and so potentially that's who she's taking the chance with, some driver who now knows where she lives or works.

It's a weird thing to be attracted to a woman and be restricted from doing what should come naturally, but it's just the wrong time to do it. Out of 30,000 trips, I've only done it three times, and I've gone 0/3, meaning nothing came of it. I got the numbers though. LOL (Pride kicked in, I had to come back and correct the record.)

One of them gave me her email address but she turned out to be a straight kook. The other one was a nurse from Alabama, and it just didn't get off the ground, and the last one offered her number while I was in a relationship. The relationship was on the rocks, and I was open – I never called or texted her. The tricky part to those interactions is that some women can give you their number as a way of survival, so they don't have to figure out how to reject you and not deal with the potential aftermath of an already vulnerable situation. It's tempting but I'd steer clear.

Chapter 18:
He Tried To Kidnap Us!

One night in Hollywood I'm passing through a side street that leads you from La Brea to Hollywood Blvd. It's where the Walk of Fame starts and to your left are only two stars, one is for Elvis, and the other is for the Beatles. To your right is/was a club. I had to yield before I merged onto Hollywood Blvd., so sometimes you see things happening outside of the club.

This night I saw two twenty-something Asian girls walking out of a club. They were inebriated and having a good time. A man who was parked on this narrow street was trying to wave them over to him. He was clearly interested, and they were not. They loudly dismissed him from just outside the club as he stood by his car. "NOOOO, WE DON'T WANT YOU! WE ALREADY HAVE SOMEBODY. GET BACK IN YOUR CAR. NOOOOOO!", almost in unison. By this time, it's my turn to merge, so I drive off.

Once I got about a block away, I received a ping for a ride. I made the right at Orange, then another right on Hawthorne then back onto La Brea, and the map was leading me back to where I had just come from. And as I pull up, I see that the same two Asian girls that I had just three minutes ago seen loudly dismissing a man... they were my passengers.

As I hit the button to let them know that I had arrived, a Prius, (the same car as mine), pulls up behind me and waved my passengers, the two Asian girls, into his car. Again, they're drunk so they don't realize that it's the same man they were just loudly dismissing minutes before.

I attempted to wave them into my car and honked the horn, but they don't see me; instead they beeline directly to the other Prius. The only thing left to do is call them, but the call goes directly to voicemail. 91

On the way in the car, one girl is in, and the other one has dropped something. I called again and this time she picked up. "Hello, I'm your Uber driver", I said. "NOOOOOOOOOO, NOOOOOOOOOO, WE'RE ALREADY IN OUR RIDE, DON'T EVEN TRY IT", she says, loudly dismissing me like she did her current driver who she does not recognize. I said, "Hey, before you hang up, how do I have your number?".

There were about two seconds of silent recalibration before she screams, "OH MY GOD, GET THE F**K OUT OF THE CAR, THIS IS THE SAME GUY FROM BEFORE", and through her yelling I can hear him trying to keep them in the car and pleading that he'd take them where they wanted to go. They scurried out of his car and into the back seat of mine. It was a quick and tense moment.

During the 20-minute trip back to Koreatown, the girls loudly thanked and praised me for alerting them to "the scammer", as they called him. When we reached their destination, they wouldn't let me leave until the boyfriend came outside so they could tell him the story. He seemed confused with a face that read, "this IS crazy but why do I have to come outside for this".

We both had a silent man-to-man, "I get it" moment and they stumbled into the lobby of their high-rise apartment building in Koreatown. I drove off and that was enough for the night.

I wonder what his plan was. Was he a driver who picked up the wrong two Asian girls or was he a rogue taxi driver trying to snag my ride and offer them a cheaper ride paid in cash? Or did he have more nefarious intentions? Hearing him getting angry because they wouldn't stay with him made me wonder if it was the latter. I hope that he wasn't a dangerous creeper but if he was, I'm glad to have helped.

Food. FOod. FOOD.

The pitfalls or joys, depending on how you look at it, of driving around this massive city every day, is having a delicious place to eat that's bad for those pounds you planned to lose. If I'm in Santa Monica on Wilshire then I know that Sidecar Donuts is near, or DK Donuts on Santa Monica Blvd also in Santa Monica, or SK Donuts on 3rd St. in LA! If I'm in Palms, then I know that the KOGI food truck by Chef Roy is on Overland. It's a Mexican/Korean fusion and their short-rib burrito is a no-brainer!

If I'm on Crenshaw, then "Not Yo Tacos" food truck is there, or if I'm in Pasadena then "Bad Ash Bakes" has the best cinnamon rolls ever! Other than those specialty spots, there are your sandwich spots all over these spread-out towns, like "Ikes" (get the Matt Cain, trust me) or Mendicino Farms (Turkey Avo and Curry Cous-Cous LAWD!!!!!) or the Short Rib sandwich at "Jones on Third"? Look, I'm down 15 lbs. in the last few months but I'm tested every single day!

I routinely recommend these places to newcomers. Burgers: Stout Burger (Hollywood) They match your burger with one of their many beers. Roscoe's Chicken and Waffles, even though they took away the Obama Special??? I won't comment on why, but y'all should fix that. Also, having no options for just one waffle, that's not cool. If you want a nice, sexy date spot with good food, check out Issa Rae's new restaurant, "Somerville", as well as "Alta", in Hollywood.

Korean BBQ; Quarters or Gangnam Station BBQ. There are so many options in K-Town, but those seem to be a few favorites among the customers. BBQ; Bludso's on La Brea and now in Santa Monica. Not as good as the OG location in Compton, but still good.

PIZZA; Masa's of Echo Park. Now, this place has other food, but for fifteen years I've only gotten their Deep Dish and it's beautiful. ITALIAN; Jon and Vinny's. Not fancy, just good food. FANCY ITALIAN; Mother Wolf. Get the Rigatoni All' Amatriciana. You're welcome! A nice low-key, good food, people watching spot is Marmalade Café at The Grove. I'll be here all day suggesting things but take those for starters. Also, Stevie's Creole Café has an amazing gumbo - and so on, and so on. LA isn't a food city? You're crazy!

Chapter 19:
Trans Persons

One night in Hollywood I pulled up to an apartment and I waited for a few minutes, and when the fare finally got to the car, there were three decent-sized women, all dressed up and ready to go out. When they got in, I see that they are all Trans Women. Now look, this was near the beginning of my time as a driver and I'm from Indiana, so besides one guy from our high school who we just thought, "wanted to be a girl", I hadn't ever really been this close to someone transitioning.

We sat in the car, me silently, them jovially as they were headed to a night on the town. There were two in back and one in the front, then the one in the front says, "you nervous, huh?", and we all burst into laughter. They could smell it on me, and for what, these are people. This is how white people treat black people, so why was I somehow nervous to interact with humans just because they were "different"? I guess it's something about certain parts of masculinity that makes us "protective", like it's going to jump off of them and splat onto us. (Maaaan, I'm gonna get some heat from this one LOL) After we laughed, I took the time to ask a question that had been debated. "So if you're turning into a man.", I asked, "Transitioning, but go ahead", she said, as we laughed again. "My bad, transitioning, and if you like men, then what is your orientation", I asked. The one in the front looked to the backseat with a familiar eyeroll and someone behind me said, "I'll take this one. If I'm a woman, that means I'm straight, duh", and they laughed again. You can tell that there had been a potent pre-game sesh. Anyway, it was a quick, fun and enlightening trip, and it released a lot of unnecessary angst toward a group of people. That even felt weird to type.

DO YOU GET TIRED OF THE RADIO?

Sometimes I do. The key is to have a variety of preset stations. I used to play music from my personal TIDAL playlist and that almost never missed. I had the main all-purpose playlist, then I had specialized playlists for the nighttime.

To continue giving a good experience, I like to profile. If you're an elderly person, I give you jazz; if you're an older person from Europe, and I can tell by the names, I'll give you classical; if you're white and in your 20s, KIIS FM, if you're black and in your 20s most likely you'll get Kday 92.3 or Power 106. If you're late 30s and black, you get KJLH, Stevie Wonder's radio station. And if you're in your 30s-50s and white, you get Rock 103.5. But my all-purpose for easy listening is 94.7 The Wave! Anita Baker, Sade, Selena, Fleetwood Mac, Return of the Mack (Stop hatin on this masterpiece), MJ, it catches everything!

Now I'm in the podcast stage and I've been there for years! At the beginning I would play my podcast episodes out loud, until I got reported twice. One was for the ending of Toure's podcast. Back then he used to end every show with, "And the man can't shut us down", and someone reported that "it was annoying". Yeah, exactly what you're thinking. The other was an episode of Death, Sex and Money. I forgot what that report was for, but after that report I stopped listening to them out loud and I got earphones.

I will say that there were many highlights from that time period. I put quite a few passengers on to a bunch of podcasts, but the crown jewel was part 2 of the Lenny Kravitz episode of *Questlove Supreme* podcast – it was a riot and the passenger kept asking me, "wait, that's Lenny Kravitz?", and "what is this, again?". They thought it was radio. Great episode. I gotta listen to that again.

I must shout out some of my favorite pods over the years; *Serial* season 1. The catalyst that brought everybody into the pod game. *In The Conversation, The Daily, Smartless, Armchair Expert, Armchair Anonymous, Bill Simmons Podcast , Conan O'Brien Needs a Friend, The Moth, How I Built This, Esther Perel, Snap Judgment, Higher Learning, Joe Budden* pod, *Rory and Mal, Knuckleheads, All the Smoke, Lovers and Friends, Freakonomics, This American Life, Criminal, Marriage Be Hard, The Thing Is, Gary Vee, We Sound Crazy, We Don't Always Agree* (COME BACK), Any Neal Brennan podcast lol, *The Right Time w/ Bomani Jones, Native Land, Denzel Washington is the Greatest Actor of All Time Period, The Big Picture, Prestige TV, Prof G* pod, *Earn Your Leisure, The Diary of a CEO, The Rewatchables, IMO With Michelle Obama* and *Craig Robinson, This Was Us, Office Ladies, Larry Wilmore Black on the Air, Heavyweights, R & B Money, Grits n Eggs, Juan Ep* (back in the day eps, tho), *Can We Talk RnB?*, WTF *Marc Maron, Screenwriters Rant Room. Renegades: Born in the USA* and *What's Your Favorite Song?*, you thought I wasn't going to shout out my own pod!? PUH! That's all I can remember for now.

Chapter 20:
80 Year-Old Former Racist

Occasionally you get a trip that warms your heart, and it restores part of your faith in humanity. The truth is that I'm black. And don't leave yet, I know you don't want to hear this, but often it's difficult being black in this country because of the same reason that makes you want to stop reading this. The older I get the more I notice racism's ugly, cunning and insidious ways. Sometimes the thing that you expect to happen doesn't happen. You must judge each case by each case, but there are very familiar patterns.

One day I had to pick up a man from LAX. He was an older white man, in his late 70s. He needed to go all the way to Calabasas, about a 30-mile, hour and a half trip depending on the time of day. The man and I started talking right away about life and work. He was a retired military lawyer who needed something to do so he picked up a new job that let him fly to a city and drive a different car back to where he lives. He was up there in age, so it was both impressive and concerning.

When we reached Calabasas, he asked: "Since you drove me all this way, can I buy you lunch?". This was a weird request, but he knew how much of a haul this was, and we'd had a great conversation and perhaps he was just being gracious. He seemed like a good man and it felt as if he wanted to talk more, so what could it hurt? Only thing I was missing out on was another hour and a half drive back to LA. Now with an 80-year-old white man and a 40-year-old black man, the conversation at some point is going to turn to race. He mentioned to me that there wasn't always a time where he and I could've had that conversation, that the only thing he knew about black people was that they weren't good.

He told me that growing up in the south, when he was in the car with his parents, he was urged to roll up his window if black people were nearby. Something like that is always jarring for me to hear because it means that if "regular" white people felt that way then how did local police, judges, corner store owners and hiring managers feel about people who looked like me, back then? That kind of racism has so many incalculably lasting effects on every generation of Blacks in America.

He said it wasn't until he had a family of his own and his son started bringing friends home to play, some of whom were black, that he considered the flaws of his upbringing. He said that he looked up and saw them playing one day and had an epiphany: "that little boy just wants to be happy.", he said. He said, "It took the joy of innocent children laughing and playing to realize that black people are just people." I know. I know.

He went on to tell me that the same son who brought black friends home to play, grew up to be a DJ and ended up getting into music but also into drugs and unfortunately, he overdosed some years back. So perhaps getting to hang out with someone his son's age was refreshing or nostalgic for him.

Once we were ready to order, a waiter came to the table with the most skeptical look on his face. He was white and it was evident that he was wondering what an 80-year-old white man and a 40-year-old black man had to talk about, but he just didn't want to say it. After we ordered the food, not able to withstand the forces of ignorance, he asks, "So tell me guys, what's really going on here?". The wording was incredible.

I had no less than eight stories to tell him about who I was, all of them set to make him feel like a shell of himself... but the good sir, the retired lawyer, was one step ahead of me and had his own rebuttal to the clueless waiter. "He's the pastor that's overseeing my wife's funeral", the former lawyer said. The waiter's demeanor changed, and he instantly became remorseful. You may think it's cruel, but I thought it was brilliant and right on time. The waiter later paid for our appetizers. The man and I finished the meal as we talked about politics, marriage and more life. Once we were finished, I took him to the dealership, and we parted ways. We never corrected the story.

HOW DO YOU DEAL WITH ROAD RAGE?

The entire body is so engaged when you're driving and it's easy to snap off and react irrationally. I've seen it happen and unfortunately, I've even had it a few times. Early on I learned to calm down immediately. I learned that there is a nano second that you have, just before you make a decision, where you have time to change that decision. It's not easy to spot but there is time, most of the time.

Also, I just try to tell myself two things; 1. How would you explain this thing escalating to an irreversible point. How would someone else explain it if you weren't here to explain it; 2. "They almost hit you, but they didn't and you're fine. Keep it moving.

See, being inconsiderate is one of my big pet peeves and a person being reckless in a two-thousand-pound vehicle, that's the height of inconsideration. To calm myself down I just imagine that they must do #2 very, very bad – we all can empathize with that. We've all been 5 minutes from disaster but 6 minutes away from the closest restroom.

So yes, there have been a few screaming matches, a chase that you've read about and an almost fight with 3 construction workers, that story I took out of the book, but it was unnecessary. I got surrounded then I got back in my car, end of story. I've learned to just breathe and smile and whatever road rage existed, will be washed away quickly if you let it.

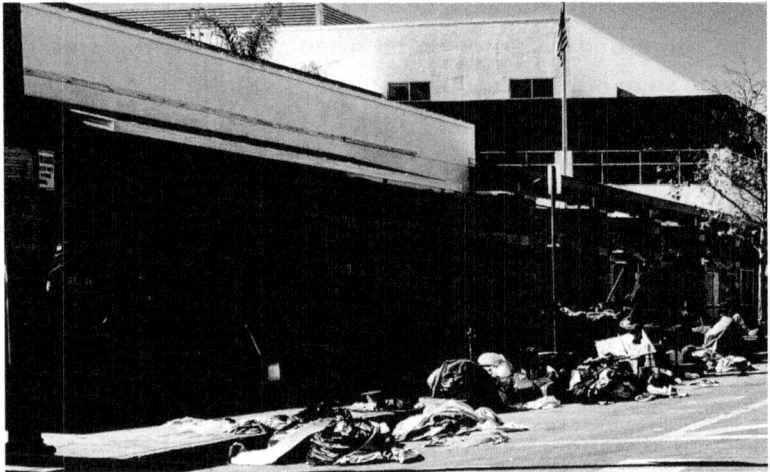

Chapter 21:
Unlucky Dog

I am not a pet guy, although there are a few dogs who have won my heart over. I had a few bad experiences with dogs when I was younger plus my Mom had a few bad experiences as well and feared them, so I guess I sort of inherited the beef. Throughout the years, dogs, (particularly one named Phoebe), have helped to soften my heart to other dogs.

One day I dropped off a few passengers at the Griffith Observatory. When you're leaving there, everything is downhill and after the winding part the straightaway is steep. If you don't watch it, you can gain quite a bit of speed on your way down. This day was no different, I had gained some speed and as I was rolling alongside the Greek Theatre, an outside concert venue (I saw Lauryn Hill and Nas there, she was on time), and there was a man in the middle of the road who had opened his door to check on something and a dog had sprung out.

Before I knew it, the dog was heading toward my car at an angle and though I tried to pull as far to the right as possible, to try and avoid hitting the dog, the dog wasn't that lucky. I felt the dog under my car as I tried to slow down. I felt awful. It all happened so fast. Before I came to a complete stop, I could see the owner running over to check on his dog.

Once I stopped, I couldn't get out of the car fast enough to see about the dog and as soon as I opened the door, the dog jumped into my car. It seems that I had only rolled the dog and missed running it over with my tires. I was so relieved! Perhaps the dog jumped in the car to escape any more cars. I'm not sure but I was, as Francene (my Mom) would put it, a happy camper. After the dog jumped in the car, it then jumped right back out and into the arms of the owner who was running to my car. 103

He leaned into my car holding the dog and apologized for what happened. The dog only had a slight scratch on its lip and was shaking from the incident. As it turned out he wasn't even the owner, he was just dog sitting. PHEW!

FUNNY MOMENTS?

My favorite song of all time is "GOODBYE LOVE", by the group GUY! Guy, along with JODECI, Mary J Blige, Al B Sure!, Father MC, Heavy D and a host of others, were signed to Uptown Records. The president of Uptown Records was Andre Harrell. (Sidenote, Andre Harrell had a talented, driven, pesky intern that he had to fire named Sean Combs).

I picked Andre up in Hollywood and I really couldn't believe it was him. Honestly, the music during his time at Uptown defined an entire generation of RnB music, even until this day. I couldn't wait to at least thank him for his contributions. When he got in the car, his mouth dropped and he said, "motherf***r you look just like Lee Daniels". It threw off the rhythm of the speech I was set to make. "Playboy has anybody ever told you how much you look like Lee Daniels?". "I'm about to call him and tell him", "If you're an actor then you need to do something with that because you look like his mf'n twin".

The trip was only about 10 minutes, but he harped on how much I looked like Lee Daniels until the moment the ride was finished. I didn't see it but that was definitely a Lee Daniels era for me because Andre, another passenger, two guys at Dunkin Donuts in Hollywood and the security guard at Roscoe's, they all thought the same thing around this time, 2017ish. Fyi I'm currently in a Timbaland/Ice Cube era - don't ask me why. I never got to tell Andre Harrell how much I appreciated his movement, but I did. His contribution to music and the culture is enormous. Rest In Peace, Andre Harrell.

Chapter 22:
Francois

Francois was a guy I picked up at about 10 a.m. one morning. He worked in accounting for a logistics company. He was pensive and seemed sad. He was French. There is often that moment when the entire ride has been quiet, and one thing shakes up the silence and causes a conversation that lasts the rest of the trip. This day it was both of us witnessing a man catching an older woman before she fell off the curb onto a busy street.

Francois had a deep accent. First, he mentioned that he was leaving a meeting, but I didn't know there to be places to meet in the place he was leaving, so my voice inflection unintentionally questioned him. We talked about food in the place that he just left. I told him that I had just recently revealed to a new woman that I was talking to, that I spoke a little (very little) French and how it was working. I also told him about how I have in the past used words like fromage, du pain and Maison to impress women while either not really knowing what I was saying or by putting words together like that weren't even sentences. After a melancholy start, he was beginning to open up. He told me how American women love the accent and how when he needs to, he exaggerates the accent even more when in their presence.

After talking about the weather, comparing French and American cuisines and how all you have to do is add more butter to make your sauces better, he revealed that he had just been in a support meeting for spouses of alcoholics. He said it like he really wanted to get it off his chest. "Is she better", I asked. "No, but I'm better", he said. "The meetings really help", he said. We ended the trip laughing about how my broken French was working and he even gave me a few more phrases to use. I'm basically fluent now.

TIMES WHERE YOU WERE IN THE WRONG.

Sometimes the trip doesn't go as planned and you wish you can have do-overs, but in a city of 12 million people, you just must live with how it happened and do better next time. The older woman who knew the neighborhood but whose directions you didn't want to take because you just don't like it, but she ended up being right, or the person who wasn't at the pickup spot and it took way too long for them to get to the car only to realize that you read the map wrong and it was you who wasn't in the right spot. Or maybe a time when you were right but went about it like a jerk and made a passenger feel bad. Yeah, there are a bunch of those that I wish I could do over.

One day in Santa Monica, I got a fare that led me to the Chevron gas station at the corner of Wilshire and 5th. As I pulled into the gas station, I see a woman unloading a car parked in front of the air pumps. Since I don't see anybody, I creep toward the other side of the gas station near where the woman was unloading a car. Surely this isn't her and surely she's not about to load all of that stuff in my car.

"Hey there, I'm the Uber driver, are you Kate?", I asked. "Yes", she said. Kate said, "my car stalled on me so I just need to grab some stuff to take with me", and as she says this, an enormous golden retriever hops out of her car, around the unbagged, loose articles of clothing and other things she was planning to put into my car. It was then that I made the decision.

"I'm sorry ma'am", I said out of the window as I pulled off. Look, I know, but sometimes you can just look at things and know they're not going to go well.

Between the dog dander that I'd have to vacuum from my seats after she was gone, to the no less than 20 loose pieces of clothing, a big a** lamp and boxes that she wanted to load into my car, this is a trip I just didn't have the capacity for.

Once I cleared the gas station, something told me to look in the back seat. I looked in the back seat. Her purse was still in the back seat. Why? And pinging on my phone is a trip that's paying just as much but for half the time and half the hassle, but I can't take it because I must give her purse back. I wanted to just hold her purse out of the window and drive with my head bowed down so that I didn't have to look her in the eye, but that would be tragic at a gas station.

I pulled back up to the station, chewing crow and with a humble smile, damn near bowing as I held the purse out of the window. "Hey there, I think you left your pur-", she snatched it before I could finish. I get that, I deserved that. To try and gain some goodwill with a woman I'll never see again, I waved at her dog on my way out. Don't ask me why. Sorry lady, but that was a lot.

Chapter 23:
My Big Break : The Writer Girl

As I've said sever times, I'm an actor and I write a little bit, TV pilots, features, but acting is what brought me to Los Angeles. One night I picked up a Caucasian woman who had been drinking but wasn't drunk. She was fun, funny and we were having a great conversation when she suddenly went quiet and she got a concerned look on her face. She just stared at me from the back seat.

I'm wondering if I'd done anything wrong. It's late, she's been drinking, we're nearing her home and it's late. This is the last place that I want a misunderstanding of any kind, I'm immediately behind the eightball. "I'm sorry, are you an actor?", she asked. "Yes, I am" I said with a shocked, how did she recognize me from the one episode of Franklin and Bash 6 years ago, tone. "Your voice is incredible, I mean it's incredible", she exclaimed. "Wow, thank you!" I said.

"I know this sounds crazy but I'm a writer for this show called (REDACTED), and the main character (Let's just call him Hustle Jordan) is going to have a Shaman, guru, spiritual mentor that he looks up to, and your voice is so soothing that I think you'd be perfect for it!" YOOOOOOO!

I'm thinking this could be my big break! I'm a fan of that show and star, and sometimes writers can have sway on casting. If she's vouching for me, this could be the break I needed to start getting into these rooms, especially since I was without an agent. "The only issue is that you'd have to fly to New York if this happens, is that ok?", she said. I told her that I'd fly myself there if I got the role. She told me to send my acting reel to her Instagram, and she gushed over my voice once more before she got out of the car. "Remember, please send it to me. I think you're perfect for the role", she said before she got out. I assured her that I would, and I drove a few houses down because I needed her to have that info pronto!

The next morning, I reached out to a woman who I knew was also a writer on that show, just as a reinforcement and hopefully to make the woman I had just met a bit more comfortable about suggesting me for the role. After that, I sent my new writer friend a follow up message on IG, and crickets... I really hate that Instagram lets you see if a person has read your message. That just shouldn't exist but I'm glad it does. She read the message and didn't say anything. I waited a couple of days, and I followed up again, and again and nothing. She read that one too. Not a "hey, sorry, somebody else got the role", or nothing. Just a read message and a non-answer. That's Hollywood.

Things like that had happened before, but I thought this time was different, you always think that, but Chinatown is Chinatown. I still follow her on IG, 6 years later... Maybe I'm hoping that she'll one day right her "wrong". I SHOULD stay her name, but in the words of Oran "Juice" Jones, "but instead, I chilled". And I should've used the Bernie Mac Kings of Comedy reference here, but my Mama is going to read this and I'm trying not to cuss. HEY MA! LOVE YOU!

DO YOU GET TIRED OF LA TRAFFIC?

Short answer, yes. I really enjoy connecting with people. I've met so many wonderful humans with so many amazing stories and personalities and honestly that gets me by from trip to trip. This LA traffic becomes white noise after a while, then it becomes annoying again at any given moment.

One time someone was on their way to my Hollywood apartment and when they described to me where they were, I said: "yeah you're about 17 minutes away", and they got quiet. "Hello", I said. "How did you guess exactly 17 minutes?", she said.

It's one of those things you just pick up when you've been driving so many miles for so long.

Oddly enough there are places that I've been dozens of times, and I still get turned around. There are other places that I feel like I don't recognize, but a corner store, a gas station or a house will jog my memory, and I'll instantly know where I am.

One weird outcome of using GPS so much is that sometimes I'll know where I'm going but I have to catch myself from still looking to the phone for the GPS. I'll be off the clock and driving home, still checking the GPS. At the end of the night, I like to catch a ride that's 29 minutes or so from my apartment. That's when I can really listen to music and that's the thing that I still enjoy, watching that LA sunset, driving down Sunset with Jon B They Don't Know, or Piece of my Love by Guy, or the full Carl Thomas Emotional album. A perfect way to cap off the day.

Chapter 24:
A Boy And His Mum

On my first ride of the day, I spot a mother and her son standing across the street from where I am, on Sunset, in front of a Philz Coffee (Really good coffee, btw). She spotted me a few seconds after I spotted her. I motioned to her with my hand to stay there and that I would come around to them. I waited for the traffic to clear, and I made the U-turn.

Once she got in the car, I heard the accent and I asked where she was from, "Bedfordshire", she said with a powerful UK accent. Claire, the mother, introduced me to her son, Tyron and for the rest of our time together, I called him, "White Tyron", because in America (and this is very niche), Tyron is usually a "Black" name. I told him he was the first white Tyron that I had ever met, and they got a kick out of that.

I learned that Claire's husband, Tyron's dad, had passed away about five or so years ago, and it was just her and her boy. Tyron has autism and the way she explained it, when he's done with something, he's done and that sometimes there was more "stimuli" than he wanted to deal with at a given time. Tyron is a smart, funny, witty lil guy well beyond his years, who needed to finish his story about whatever the topic was. It was amazing to watch her work with him, to watch her let him finish a story or a thought about something, even when she didn't "want" to, or had something to say.

Anyway, Claire had asked Tyron where on the map he wanted to go, and he said "LA". One of the places he wanted to visit was Target. He wanted to visit other places and see other media-familiar parts of America, but Target was one of them.

I dropped them off and I told them I'd be writing a book, and Claire suggested that we'd laughed enough that she thought they had a shot at making the book. At that time, though we had "had a laugh", I had not planned to put them in the book.

The next day while on Hollywood Blvd, just east of La Brea, I'm headed west and who do I spot except Tyron and Claire, walking the opposite way. There weren't any cars behind me, so I had time to pull closer to them while pointing directly at them. White Tyron spotted me immediately and alerted his mother Claire.

Now, having been raised by my mom, sights like this just tug at my heartstrings and I kick in to "how can I help" mode. I shouted, "do you need a ride anywhere?", she shouted back, "Target, in one hour. Is that okay?", I said, "I'll see you in one hour". They were about a block or so from Target at the time. So I plotted out my rides, making sure I didn't get too far away and when the time came, I pulled up to Target just as they were walking out. I took them back to their hotel in the valley.

We exchanged numbers and I told her, "while you're here, and if I can, I'll take you where you need to go". Before they got out, Claire offered me money and I declined, because I just wanted to be of service. She wouldn't think of it, and she made me take the money. I would take them to three or four more places, including the airport, and each time she would give me more money than the ride would've cost, which was really not my intent.

I understand what she was doing, but it was hard to accept. I even tried to slide some money off to Tyron in the back seat, and literally behind Claire's back, but she caught me and was rather annoyed. "Listen, I get what I want. Just take the money". She said it in such a tone and with such a serious expression, that I stopped fighting.

We learned about each other's culture. I told them about the stories that hopefully you've already read (lol). They were fascinated by our stop signs and who was supposed to go first. They taught me phrases, one of which was "having a laugh", and a few more tawdry ones that I can't say out loud (LOL) All in all, when it was time to take them to LAX, we had spent so much of that short time together, that a part of me felt sad when it was time for them to go. We laughed and learned, and Tyron shared these amazing marshmallow shrimp candies with me, TWO BAGS that I devoured when I discovered them in my glove compartment a few days later.

Both Tyron and I were well-behaved children being taken care of by a mother who was a force of nature. It felt familiar and I was glad to help. I'm glad to have met them. I hope they're doing well.

WHITE-TYRON, THE BOOK IS OUT IN LESS THAN 365 DAYS!!!!!!! THANKS FOR THAT PRESSURE, MATE! LOL

GOALS

Staying in LA presents a different type of challenge than thriving in LA. When I moved here, I was 27 and it was just about working midnights at Target on La Brea and Rodeo (now Obama Blvd), overnights from 10pm to 6am.

I would come home and sleep until about 1pm then go audition for terrible plays, short films and student-directed scenes of already famous movies. (My first one was The big scene from Heat. Twas awful) That was the life!

A couple years and jobs later, I started a courier service called "ALL AROUND COURIER", and a I made a website, got a DBA and with no marketing I started getting calls. This came at the end of a nine-month long unemployment streak and just as the calls started coming in for this courier service, a job that I applied for called me in. What to do, what to do. Unfortunately, I chose the comfort of a steady check. Damn. Considering how I'd eventually complete 30k trips with Uber/Lyft and 2k deliveries with Task Rabbit, Uber and Amazon, it seems that I made the wrong call.

Then there was the time when I was buying and selling items through a program called Amazon FBA. I would source the items through different websites or stores then itemize and tag them, then send them to Amazon to sell. In turn they would take a percentage of the sales but handle all the customer service, packaging and shipping. It was a sweet deal if you knew what you were doing. I remember getting this mini load of different kinds of items, a third of it sold, another portion of the items I wasn't allowed to sell on Amazon due to copyright issues, and the third set of items was a Milwaukee Tools fence repair kit, but it sold out immediately. I remember being surprised by it, but I was also bummed out about the things that didn't sell.

I clearly put the wrong energy into the wrong things. Also, not really knowing the retail game as well, I remember not being enthused about the margins, even though I had a perfect setup.

So instead of doubling down on those Milwaukee Tool fence repair kits, I let the account go. TILL THIS DAY I'm not sure why.

After that came a vending debacle, several attempts at selling T-shirts online, none of which stuck around for too long. The most promising attempt came just recently, but unfortunately, I was too ambitious (copyright), and Etsy has banned me for life from selling. (LOL Damn, Coldplay and 3K) Hopefully we can fix that, but it doesn't look good. My bad, Etsy!

I've tried even more things than I've written here. The goal has always been acting in TV and film but I've also always aspired to start my own businesses and that part has proven to be tough – but we're not done. So many options, and honestly, I'm guilty of a great deal of procrastination as well as analysis paralysis. I'm narrowed down now and irons are for real in the fire.

CCS
Continental
MAS POR MENOS
PRECIOS DE DESCUENTO
VIAJES
213.413.5494
4 LESS
ADELANTADO ATM
TOURS
2100
DIAGONAL CROSSING
OK

Chapter 25:
Everywhere Reminds Me Of Everything

One of the other issues of having been here so long and having driven around so much is remembering where certain events were and remembering the people you shared those moments with. If I'm in Echo Park, I'm remembering a surprise party thrown for me by a woman I was dating at Masa's of Echo Park, or the Echoplex where I've attended many "Soul Slams" and "Wonderful" parties, with my people.

If I'm on Venice and Cochran I remember receiving the call that "Gunny", my maternal grandmother had passed away on June 9th, 2016. If I'm deep into the valley on Ventura, I remember the restaurant I was at where I waited for David Arquette for 10 minutes and he gave me a $20 cash tip in 2016. I remember the corner of Highland and Melrose where, at a stop light, I convinced a young lady to share her popcorn with me. I never thought she'd say yes, but at the red light she got out of the car and poured popcorn in my hands! We both laughed with and at each other for the next few lights.

When I'm near Dodger Stadium I'm remembering being in line to get in the game with my dear friend Bryce Fluellen in 2022 and as we're going in, Denzel Washington walks out of the gate. We were both trippin the randomness of LA. Bryce, a father, a husband, master chef, entrepreneur and food activist, passed away on January 1st, 2024. He's the one who inspired me to write a book just as he did a few years back, "FOOD. A Vehicle for Healing. (The Fruitful Journey) Part. 1".

If I'm in Studio City and I pass Vivians Café, I think about the time that Sherrie, April, and I ate there like we would from time to time, and I offered to pay for everybody's meal. They made a huge deal out of it, exclaiming that I never treat them. Just after I paid, a reality show producer who was scouting the restaurant for a shoot, offered to pay for our meals because she was shooting some video in our direction. I was EVEN STEVEN, and my dear friends were undone.

Ansherria Jenkins, a wonderful, dynamic, NAACP Award winning producer for the Steve Harvey talk show, Iyanla Vanzant "Fix My Life", TD Jakes talk show, The Doctors, and countless others, passed away on September 21st, 2021. She left behind her parents, a sister and a football team of cousins and friends who loved her. She used to call me Rain Man. (LOL) We pitched a movie together at TVONE, back in 2018. We met in an acting class at Tennessee State University!

Part of being a driver allows you to be flexible enough to go to an audition or to come pick up Thin Mint Girl Scout cookies that your friend April Atwater ordered for you against your will. "NOPE! Come get these cookies", April exclaimed when I tried to resist. "April, you know what I'm going to do to those cookies", I said. "I have an audition around 12, meet me at Ralph's on Third and La Brea", she said. I pulled into the parking lot, and I walked to meet her just to the left of the main doors. She handed me the cookies and like always we couldn't just say "what up", and leave. We talked for about 40 minutes. We talked about auditions, life, and the MARTIN show as we always did. April asked me, "how long you think it'll take you to eat those cookies", I said "about six weeks", "Umm Tatuhs", she said. That meant she didn't believe you!

She was right. I left April for what would be the last time, as she was reminded that she needed to buy something from Ralph's.

I did immediate damage to the first sleeve of the Thin Mints. I sent April a text about an hour later showing her the remnants of the crumpled, plastic sleeve that once held the cookies. She laughed and texted back, "I told you".

Unfortunately, April passed away suddenly, three days later. I had a passenger in the car when I got the news. I pass by Ralph's grocery store every single day. Over two years later and I still can't bring myself to eat the other sleeve of Thin Mints. They're still in the freezer. April, Sherrie and I would gather at Sherrie's apartment several times a month for at least 10 years. I miss them.

Chapter 26:
In Conclusion

To all impatient, obnoxious and horn-honking drivers who are the sixth car from the light, who will never ever make the light but still cause high stress levels for everyone else, I wish you phantom speeding tickets cameras. You make driving in the streets of Los Angeles scary and dangerous. Stop.

I wish all my fellow drivers prosperity. I wish you the best in whatever you strive to do after you're out of the seat. I wish you free car washes, vacuums and air fresheners for life. I wish you low gas prices and the highest gas mileage allowable. I wish you peaceful passengers and easy, high-paying routes. I wish solidarity to the point of having NO MORE rides under $5 (Everyday, not just Fridays LOL). I wish you quiet passengers without their own "better route". I hope you're looking for and end up making it to that "next thing", whatever it may be.

To all my passengers, I'm glad to have shared my space with you. You've taught me about humanity, forgiveness, patience and humility. Even you impatient, rude ones, thanks. Human beings are everything. We're temperamental, we're egotistical, we're hard-headed, we're perfectly imperfect.

Human nature is the only class that we'll have to take over and over again until we're out of here, so we might as well learn as much as we can about how to deal with each other, and most importantly how to deal with ourselves.

Thank you for those lessons. My name is David Ashley, and these were the Confessions of a Hollywood Uber Driver.

AKNOWLEDGMENTS

I'd like to thank my Mother. Thank you for your everlasting support. You've been through a lot, we've been through a lot, and I couldn't have made any of this happen without your love and support. "What's up with the book, man?", you would ask me every few weeks or so, and you kept me to my word. I love you more than words can say. YOU GET THE FIRST COPY!!!!!!!!!!!!!!!!!!!!!!!!!!!!!!!!!

Thank you goes to fellow authors Rae Karim, Acamea Deadwiler, Kenny Young, Maryland Thomas and of course Bryce Fluellen. They have all self-published and have added to this journey inspirationally.

Thank you to Luba! You are a God send! Thank you for your selflessness and your confidence in me. She went by one name long before Cher!

I want to also thank my friends, family and Fram for letting me rant about any of these stories on any given conversation. To my Facebook friends, thank you for complimenting me on my storytelling. Years ago, on some long and drawn-out story I wrote, one of you asked, "when is the book coming?" and it sparked something that I didn't know was there. Thank you all!

My first time telling stories was at the Young Author's Conference in Hammond, Indiana. I was in elementary school, and somebody saw fit to sign me up for the event. In the third grade there was The Greatest Dunker, in the fourth grade it was The 12 Annual Dunk Contest (notice a theme here? Lol) and in the fifth grade there was The Case of the Missing Piece of Pizza. It wasn't until I was in LA for 10 years before I realized how long I'd been telling stories. So, shout out to you and I hope that you're still encouraging children and teens alike to tell stories. Thank you for existing.

About the author

David Ashley is an actor and writer from Hammond, Indiana. He has appeared in several commercials, television shows and films, and has also written and directed three short films.

Confessions of a Hollywood Uber Driver is his first book, drawing on his 30,000 trips behind the wheel as an Uber driver in Los Angeles. Customers always seemed fascinated by the stories he would tell so he decided to share them with the world.

Someone once asked Spike Lee how he wanted to be remembered, and Spike answered "He was a storyteller". David greatly identified with that statement.

Connect with the author

David Ashley also speaks at schools, film programs and community events about creativity, storytelling and finding your voice. To inquire about speaking engagements or to purchase another copy, scan the QR code:

Printed in Dunstable, United Kingdom

72279453R00078